GCSE Drama Study Guide

EDEXCEL

Kelly McManus
and
Andrew Pullen

R·

Rhinegold Education
239-241 Shaftesbury Avenue
London WC2H 8TF
Telephone: 020 7333 1720
Fax: 020 7333 1765
www.rhinegold.co.uk

Drama Study Guides
AS and A2 Drama Study Guide (Edexcel)
AS and A2 Drama Study Guide (AQA)

Music Study Guides
GCSE, AS and A2 Music Study Guides (AQA, Edexcel and OCR)
GCSE, AS and A2 Music Listening Tests (AQA, Edexcel and OCR)
GCSE Music Study Guide (WJEC)
GCSE Music Listening Tests (WJEC)
AS/A2 Music Technology Study Guide (Edexcel)
AS/A2 Music Technology Listening Test (Edexcel)
Revision Guides for GCSE (AQA, Edexcel and OCR), AS and A2 Music (AQA and Edexcel)

Also available from Rhinegold Education
Key Stage 3 Elements
Key Stage 3 Listening Tests: Book 1 and Book 2
AS and A2 Music Harmony Workbooks
GCSE and AS Music Composition Workbooks
GCSE and AS Music Literacy Workbooks
Baroque Music in Focus, Romanticism in Focus, Modernism in Focus,
Batman in Focus, *Goldfinger* in Focus, *Immaculate Collection* in Focus, *Who's Next* in Focus,
Film Music in Focus, Musicals in Focus

Rhinegold Publishing also publishes Choir & Organ, Classical Music, Classroom Music, Early Music Today, International Piano, Music Teacher, Opera Now, Piano, The Singer, Teaching Drama, British and International Music Yearbook, British Performing Arts Yearbook, British Music Education Yearbook, Rhinegold Dictionary of Music in Sound.

First published 2009 in Great Britain by
Rhinegold Publishing Limited
239–241 Shaftesbury Avenue
London WC2H 8TF
Telephone: 020 7333 1720
Fax: 020 7333 1765
www.rhinegold.co.uk

You should always check the current requirements of the examination, since these may change. Copies of the Edexcel specification may be obtained from Edexcel Publications, Adamsway, Mansfield, Notts, NG18 4FN.

Telephone: 01623 467 467, Fax: 01623 450 481, Email: publications@linneydirect.com

See also the Edexcel website at www.edexcel.com

Edexcel GCSE Drama Study Guide
British Library Cataloguing in Publication Data.
A catalogue record for this book is available from the British Library.
ISBN 978-1-906178-80-2

Printed in Great Britain by Headley Brothers Ltd

CONTENTS

THE AUTHORS

Andrew Pullen studied drama at The University of Kent in Canterbury and trained to be a teacher with Margaret Higgins at Bispham Arts College in Blackpool. He has been head of drama and performing arts at a number of schools and colleges across the south of England, and continues to work as a freelance director.

Andrew was co-artistic director of the Thorndike Exchange, a youth and community theatre company, working from the Thorndike Theatre in Leatherhead before establishing Theatre Exchange as an independent theatre company in its own right. With Theatre Exchange, Andrew developed many theatre experiences for a whole range of educational environments from primary school students to the field of disability arts. Andrew has worked as an associate drama consultant for 4S, working with Surrey LEA to develop gifted and talented provision for Year 7–11 drama students and has recently curated work for the Surrey Youth Theatre network.

Kelly McManus graduated from Dartington College of Arts with a degree in Theatre Arts. She then studied at Middlesex University and GITIS Academy in Moscow, where she gained her masters degree in theatre directing. She has combined her knowledge and experience as a director with her passion for education and teaching. She has been a head of drama in a number of schools across the south of England as well as being an advanced skills teacher. She works extensively training teachers and as an advisor for Reading University PGCE drama course. She is currently a deputy leader of expressive arts and associate director of Initial Teacher Training, studying for an EdD (Doctorate in Education) at Bath University and continues to work as a freelance director.

ACKNOWLEDGEMENTS

In the writing of a guide such as this many people have contributed. The authors and publishers are grateful to the following people for their specific advice, support and expert contributions: Margaret Higgins and Tony Grady (for inspiration at the beginning of our teaching experience and for our introduction to the work of Nick Davies), Verity Suter, Debbie Lawrence and Steve Cordwent, Lauren Arthur, Chevy Welsh, Helen Okoth, Lucy Pegg , Jason Housecroft, Leighton Carter, Anne and Mike King, Wet Picnic Theatre Company, Alan Perks, Skip Mort, Ben Robbins, Ben Smith, Lucien Jenkins and our mums and dads, and of course all the students we have worked with whose ideas and input have shaped our work.

The authors are also conscious of having drawn on a lifetime's reading. More recently the growth in use of the internet has made an unparalleled amount of exciting information and challenging opinion widely available. Although every attempt has been made to acknowledge both the primary and secondary sources drawn on, it is impossible to do justice to the full range of material that has shaped the creation of this book. The authors would therefore like to apologise if anyone's work has not been properly acknowledged. They would be happy to hear from authors or publishers so that any such errors or omissions may be rectified in future editions.

CREDIT NOTICES

You are lucky. You are about to study drama as an exam subject, and what an exciting and dynamic course you have ahead of you. This book will lead you through the Edexcel GCSE Drama course and will give you ideas, exercises, thoughts and questions to add to what you are already doing in the classroom with your group and your teacher to ensure that you get the most out of your dramatic work and also get the best grade you can achieve. What is offered here is extra help; most work will be done in your classroom alongside other people. You could follow what is written here to produce exciting practical work in your own classroom. You could read this book outside of the classroom to help you improve your level of thinking and deepen your understanding to take back into the work you are doing with your teacher and to ensure you get a better grade in your Drama GCSE.

GCSE Drama allows you to step into the shoes of anyone from the entire sweep of human history to question what their lives were like and to take these ideas back to our world today. Drama is about asking questions and then finding ways to explore the answers through performance. Keep asking lots of questions throughout your study of drama.

GCSE Drama involves exploring ideas, thoughts and feelings through making drama, performing drama and through evaluating other people's work.

You will explore ideas and put yourself in other people's shoes. You will learn what techniques are best to employ in different situations — techniques such as hot-seating, frozen images, thought-tracking and working in role.

You will then learn how to communicate what you have discovered to an audience thinking about elements such as lighting, sound, proxemics, use of set and significant props.

You will learn about plays and how playwrights communicate meaning to an audience. You will also learn how to take the words on a page and turn them into exciting and dynamic pieces of theatre.

Drama is a practical subject and, in keeping with this, all the assessment on this course is either practical or comes from practical work. You will be marked on what you do in the classroom and how you perform in plays. You will also be marked on the way you are able to write about your own and other people's practical work. You need to be able to analyse and assess your own work.

The GCSE in Drama is an exciting and rewarding course, you will work practically with other students in your class, and you will become very close to them as you produce some excellent explorative work in Units 1 and 2. You will be enormously proud of the practical work you produce for Unit 3. You will work hard, but the rewards will be enormous. Enjoy your GCSE course and good luck!

Why is it like that?
What could change?
Who caused that?
■ What has this got to do with my life and the world today?
What are the links between their lives and mine?

Why has the playwright written about this?
What is the playwright trying to say to their audience?
How can I communicate this meaning to an audience?
■ In what other ways could I use these words on a page and turn them into performance?

Why did you do that?
Could it have been done another way?
What effect did that have on the audience?
What is the context of your drama?

This book will lead you through the three Units of the Edexcel Drama GCSE:

- Unit 1: Drama Exploration
- Unit 2: Exploring Play Texts
- Unit 3: Drama Performance.

Boxes like this will appear in the margins of most pages. These boxes will give you additional information and more to think about. In this book, Unit 1 focuses on work about *Dark Heart*, Unit 2 looks at a play text called *Equus*.

Developing your thinking

Boxes like this will appear on some of the project pages. These boxes will offer you ideas about how to take the work you are doing further, and how to develop the work you are doing to ensure you improve your grade. One way of developing your understanding about this course straight away is to look at all the information about it on the exam board's website: www.edexcel.com/gcse2009 and then search for drama.

Thinking questions are used particularly in Unit 1 and Unit 2. To get good marks in these units you will need to develop your responses and thinking questions will help you do that. Thinking questions are linked to the specific work you are completing on a project page, but you could use the same types of question to develop your responses to any work you produce with your teacher.

Think tank

Think tank boxes appear throughout this book. These boxes will give you ideas about how to use the drama techniques and ideas discussed and apply them to whatever drama you are doing in your own classroom. Usually the think tank ideas are bigger ideas that move beyond the work you are completing on the project page, and suggest ways of working and ideas for developing your drama work further. All the ideas and techniques discussed in this book could apply to any drama or any play that you are studying with your teacher. It is important that you do your own reading and your own research if you want to get a top grade in this subject.

NOTEBOOKS

Keep a drama notebook. You will have to write about all the practical work you undertake for Units 1 and 2. Keep a notebook as you go along; do not leave the writing until the last minute.

Throughout this book there are a lot of thinking questions. Make sure you write your answers down to these questions, but also note down answers that were given by other people in your class.

Note down all the techniques you use in a drama performance. Also note down why you have used them and what effect they had on your audience.

When you watch other people perform, make sure you make a note about the techniques they used and the effect they had on you as an audience member.

The written work you complete for Units 1 and 2 is called the documentary response. This is written work that reflects on your own work and the work of other people in your class. In the documentary response, you will evaluate the work you have completed, as well as discussing and evaluating the way you presented your drama and the techniques you used.

It is important you become a reflective practitioner. Someone who makes excellent drama but also someone who knows:

- How they made the drama
- What techniques they used and why
- What effect they hoped to have on an audience
- The effect they did have on an audience
- What they would do differently.

GETTING GOOD GRADES – WHERE ARE YOU?

Are you here?	You should be aiming for
I know what techniques to use when I make my drama	I am also able to say what I think about the issues we are exploring
I know how I want to communicate meaning to my audience	I know why I want to communicate in the way that I do
I can tell my teacher what techniques I am using	I can discuss with my teacher the effect I hope these techniques will have on my audience
My teacher can describe techniques and I can then include them in my performance	I am able to add new techniques that my teacher hasn't mentioned into my performance work and know the effect I am hoping to achieve
I can discuss my immediate responses to a piece of drama that I watch	I can link the drama that I have seen to the bigger questions we are exploring
I know why playwrights choose the techniques that they do	I can give reasons for playwrights' choices and suggest other techniques they could have employed
I can tell my teacher what techniques were used in a performance	I can tell my teacher why certain techniques were used in performance
I can describe what I saw on stage	I can say why the actors did what they did
I can discuss what I saw and what techniques they employed and why	I spell key words correctly, my sentences are legible and my grammar is correct
I can draw links between techniques and different practitioners.	I can discuss the effect the practitioners were attempting to create and the reasoning behind the creation of those techniques.

REMEMBER TO P.E.E. ON YOUR WORK

This technique is useful for all the written work you complete, but is discussed again in the section that focuses on the written work that you complete, which is an evaluation of a live performance you see, on pages 78 to 88.

Your teacher may have a different way of you remembering this format, but one that may stick in your mind is to PEE on your work:

P	Make your point	(I thought this ...)
E	Give your example or evidence	(This is why I thought it, here is the proof)
E	Give your evaluation	(This is why it worked or why it didn't work.)

A SUMMARY OF THE SPECIFICATION

The key to success is to know each step and, therefore, know how to make the right decisions. Here is an outline of the GCSE Edexcel Drama course that you will be studying. Read all of the units carefully and pay attention to the requirements for each unit.

The GCSE examination is divided into three units.

 Drama explorative strategies are techniques that you use to investigate the meaning and reasons behind why a moment of character development or a scene is taking place. **Drama mediums** are techniques you use to communicate your interpretations of a text or stimuli to an audience. To revise the strategies and mediums turn to page 12.

UNIT 1: DRAMA EXPLORATION (6 HOURS PRACTICAL WORK)

■ In your drama lessons you will use both explorative strategies and drama mediums to explore themes, topics and issues that have been decided by your teacher. Through using drama mediums and strategies you will devise your own drama.

Your teacher will offer a variety of **stimuli** from different times and cultures that you will work on in class. These will be based on themes, topics or issues and you will make connections between them.

The learning curve

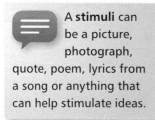 A **stimuli** can be a picture, photograph, quote, poem, lyrics from a song or anything that can help stimulate ideas.

Unit 1 focuses more on the way you put your drama together, rather than the final performance. You will be continually assessed in class by your teacher. You will take notes after each session to help form your final written documentary response of 2,000 words. This will be completed in class time under supervision.

See page 10-12 for more detail on how to write your documentary response.

UNIT 2: EXPLORING PLAY TEXTS (6 HOURS OF PRACTICAL WORK)

This unit contains two sections; one is to read and understand a play of your teacher's choice and the other is to see a live performance where you will write a critical review.

The facts

■ You will read and study a play that has been chosen by your teacher
■ You will explore the way the play has been written and question the impact it would have on an audience

> When it comes to writing about theatre you will need to avoid descriptive language: 'I went to see this play and it was really good.' See page 78 to 88 for methods of getting the top marks.

- You will analyse (unpick) the playwright's intentions and discover the deeper meanings beneath the text, characters and context
- You will respond, reflect and evaluate on the themes and issues that the play deals with, as well as developing your performance skills
- You will see a live performance of a play either in your school or at the theatre that you will write a 2,000-word critical review on.

UNIT 3: DRAMA PERFORMANCE

This is the final unit of the examination. You will use and implement what you have learnt from Units 1 and 2 to help you get the best grade. Unit 3 is assessed on performance.

You have the choice to show your talent through **performing** or as a **performance-support** candidate (costume design, make-up, lighting, set or sound design). When you need to make this decision, your teacher will be there to guide you.

What will you do?

- You will work in a small group and devise a live performance (or light, costume, make-up or set design for the group)
- Using your drama explorative strategies, you will rehearse the performance so that it is polished and ready for an audience
- You will have decided on the most appropriate drama mediums to use so your performance communicates your chosen meaning.

HOW AM I ASSESSED?

> Your teacher will assess you in class for a maximum of six hours. You will need to communicate your responses to the stimuli that your teacher prepares and presents to you. You will work in small groups and develop drama using the drama mediums and explorative strategies that you have learned. You will also get a chance to perform in front of your peers.

ASSESSMENT OVERVIEW

Unit 1	This is worth 30%
Drama Exploration	60 marks overall 40 = practical work 20 = documentary response.

Unit 2	This is worth 30%
Exploring Play Texts	60 marks overall 30 = practical work 10 = documentary response.
Response to Live Theatre	20 = response to live performance.

An aspect you may highlight in your review is the way the actors used the setting, costume, or lighting to communicate their characters' journey. You may want to look at one actor's performance in detail and write about how they changed across the play. Whatever your chosen focus is, make sure you take a note pad to record your thoughts in the theatre.

Your teacher may arrange for you to visit a theatre and see a live performance. Remember to take a note pad and try to purchase a programme so that you can read the director's intentions and refer to actors by name when you write up your review. When you are watching the play you can decide to focus on one aspect. Look at the marks awarded to this section – this tells you that the examiner is looking for a detailed account of the live performance.

Unit 3	This is worth 40%
Drama Performance	80 marks overall 20 = voice and movement 20 = role and characterisation 20 = communication 20 = content, style and form.

DOCUMENTARY RESPONSE – THE WRITTEN WORK

All of the written work that you complete for your GCSE examination will be completed under what is called controlled conditions. This means that the work you complete both practically and written will be marked and assessed under supervision.

You will be given time in class to write down:

- Your responses to the stimuli or play text
- Your ideas for how you have applied your drama explorative strategies
- Your evaluation of the drama mediums you have used.

Your teacher will allocate time to write your documentary response in class. Remember this is writing *your* opinion on what you have been doing in class. It does not have to be in essay format. You can use a variety of methods to communicate to the examiner the processes that you have been through. Look at the writing frame and examples below to help you begin your very own documentary response.

UNIT 1: DOCUMENTARY RESPONSE: UP TO 2,000 WORDS

Your documentary response to Unit 1 should consist of your opinions about the main themes that you have studied. You should communicate to the examiner your response to the work that you have been exploring in class. It is important that you use images and illustrations to express your thoughts.

Following your response you will then need to document the ways in which you have developed your drama from a range of stimuli.

UNIT 2: DOCUMENTARY RESPONSE: UP TO 1,000 WORDS

This documentary response for Unit 2 will be different to the one that you will write for Unit 1. You will have to study a play text and write about your understanding of the playwright's intentions. Keep notes in lessons and remember to put page numbers from the script so that you can easily return back to that section where you are writing your documentary response.

For example, you could stick a poem into your work and write around it what you decided as a director, designer, performer or deviser, what decisions you made, and how and why you chose the action for your production. Remember, you need to clearly communicate the scenes that you rejected and explain why you chose to reject them using your drama terminology.

Begin by recording your initial response to the play's main themes and issues. Write down what your thoughts are about the genre, structure and plot. Comment on how you think the play links to the world today and draw any comparisons to other plays, books, songs or literature that you have read.

Finally, you will need to evaluate the tasks that you completed in class and write about your most successful decisions and how they impacted on your audience.

UNIT 2: RESPONSE TO LIVE THEATRE: UP TO 2,000 WORDS

After each of the sessions your teacher may give you some time to make notes. These can be expanded upon outside of class hours but your final documentary response, which is recommended to take between two and four hours, will be completed and handed in during class time.

WHERE TO START?

For your GCSE assessment, you are required to produce two written documentary responses. These are not essays and could include:

- Brainstorms
- Roles on the wall
- Drawings, illustrations, graphics
- Writing in role
- Storyboards
- Set designs.

WHAT WRITING DO YOU NEED TO DO?

For Unit 1, your documentary response is 2,000 words.

You may be taken to see a live production by your school, family or friends. Either way you will need to be detailed and clear as the examiner may not have seen the piece you are writing about.

For Unit 2, there are two sections; your documentary response is 1,000 words long *and* your response to a piece of live theatre is 2,000 words long.

Marking: what the examiner wants to read ...

The examiner is looking for the quality of your written communication. In an excellent response, 'there is an outstanding application of written communication. Spelling, punctuation and grammar are faultless and the selected form and style are appropriate.'

Your written work is confirmation of your learning, progress and thoughts about the content of your class work that you have completed.

Explorative strategies are techniques that you will use to reflect upon and deepen your understanding of your drama. They will help you develop your understanding about characters, the themes you are exploring and the questions you are asking. You will need to evaluate how each strategy helped you gain greater insight into your enquiry.

THE EXPLORATIVE STRATEGIES

In this section we detail examples of the drama explorative strategies. The exam board says you must use at least four in Unit 1 and four in Unit 2.

What is important is that you don't just know the word and the definition. What is important is that these strategies become something that you do when you are exploring through drama. Your teacher may suggest strategies for you to use, but you may also make your own choices about the strategies you employ in your work.

Below we take a look at some of the explorative strategies. Page 14 of the Edexcel GCSE specification will show you the full list. It is important to remember you do not have to use all of the strategies but you must use at least four in each unit.

Tick the boxes in the grids once you have read the definition. Come back and check this grid as you use each strategy. Only once you have chosen to use these strategies will you begin to understand them. Come back and re-tick this grid at that point.

Strategy	Definition	I have read	I have used	I have understood
Still image	Sometimes known as a tableaux. A more advanced way of referring to this strategy is as a 'depiction'. The action is frozen like a photograph. A still image can allow us to stop the action and to reflect on a specific moment that is frozen. A still image may also be used as a starting point for the drama. Your teacher may ask you to bring the still image to life, or they may ask you to speak the thoughts of the characters in the still image. Think about titling your still image to suggest the political or cultural message that it might contain.			

Strategy	Definition	I have read	I have used	I have understood
Thought-tracking	You will always thought track as a character. When the role-play is frozen, or a still image is created, you speak the thought in the character's head. You could thought track yourself or an outside eye could step in and thought track a character.			

Think tank

This is a useful strategy to take into performance. It is always exciting when a character's inner voice is heard. (See the discussion of Artaud on pages 20 to 22 for more on this technique.) They often reveal the truth at that point. You could have another actor speaking the thoughts of a character or the character could step out of role and speak their thoughts directly to the audience. (See the discussion of Brecht on pages 25 to 27 for more on this technique.)

Strategy	Definition	I have read	I have used	I have understood
Hot-seating	As an actor you work in role and answer questions about yourself. Hot-seating helps to build up information about a role. What is important for you as an actor is to be in role when you answer the questions, rather than just speaking the answers from the character's point of view, when you are being that character; for example there may be some questions your character will refuse to answer.			

Strategy	Definition	I have read	I have used	I have understood
Forum theatre	As an audience member, you make up the forum, the forum being the audience that is watching a piece of theatre. When you think you could change the action or react differently you say 'freeze' and then step into a role taking the place of another actor. In this way, the group watching can enter the scene as any character or they can stop a scene and take over a role.			

Developing your thinking

Can you write a definition for the other explorative strategies, such as narrating, role play, cross-cutting, or marking the moment?

Think tank

There are many other explorative strategies that we will explore throughout this book. These include working in role, adopting the stance of a character, cross-cutting when you jump between different scenes building a montage. There will also be times in your dramas when you recognise an important or defining section. You may mark these moments by still image, by focusing in on a couple of lines of dialogue or by focusing in on a character. What is important is your understanding of why you are using these strategies and what they help you to understand.

Developing your thinking

Can you write a definition for the other drama mediums, including masks or make-up, sound and music, lighting, set, movement, mime and gesture, and spoken language? Reading the design skills resource pack that accompanies this book will help you with this. See this book's product page at www.rhinegold.co.uk

THE DRAMA MEDIUMS

Here are some examples of how drama mediums can be used. The exam board says you must use at least two examples of the drama mediums in Unit 1 and two in Unit 2.

Over the next few pages we consider some of the Edexcel GCSE drama mediums. Page 14 of the Edexcel GCSE specification will show you the full list. It is important to remember that you do not have to use all of the mediums of drama, but you must use at least two in each unit.

Tick these boxes in the drama medium grids once you have read the definition. Come back and check the grids as you use each medium. Only once you have chosen to use these mediums you will begin to understand them. Come back and re-tick the relevant grid at that point.

The **drama mediums** are the techniques that we usually think about when we move into performance and theatre. Drama in the classroom helps us to explore themes, issues and the bigger questions. When we move to perform drama to an audience, we look to the drama medium as a way of enhancing the communication of the meaning to our audience. All these techniques are not just single techniques that you will use in isolation. What is important when you are creating complex drama that has depth of understanding is that all the techniques are working together harmoniously to communicate meaning to your audience.

Medium	Definition	I have read	I have used	I have understood
Costume	This drama medium includes all the clothes and accessories that an actor will wear to communicate meaning to an audience. Even if you do not have access to a store of costumes, always try and think about one significant accessory that a character could wear to communicate a particular message to an audience. Think about when the play is set, the context – where the play is set – and then what you want the audience to understand about the character.			

When you are exploring your character, you could collect photographs and images on a mood board. On your mood board also think about showing colour symbolically. You might also include examples of textures that link with the character. This mood board could be the starting point for costume.

Medium	Definition	I have read	I have used	I have understood
Space and/or levels	Think about the proxemics of your scene – where you place characters in the space to sign meaning to an audience. Also think about the use of height to communicate meaning. The simplest example of this is placing someone proxemically higher to sign higher status. The position a character takes in relation to the acting area and the audience can be used symbolically.			

It is always useful to have levels as part of your design as this allows you to create meaning through proxemics. Think about the changing status of characters and how you could reflect this through changing positions on stage.

Medium	Definition	I have read	I have used	I have understood
Voice	As an actor you essentially have your body and your voice as ways of communicating with your audience. You will use vocal techniques, such as pauses, pace, volume and accents, to communicate meaning to an audience; for example, when the actor pauses it draws the audience's attention to what they have just heard and makes them wonder what will be said next. Pauses also give the impression that the character is taking time to think about what they are saying. This makes them seem more 'real'. Remember to focus on your projection – the audience need to be able to hear what you are saying.			

Chose a speech from a play you are working on. Identify where pauses might be effective. Consider what your character is signing to the audience through the use of pause and silence.

Medium	Definition	I have read	I have used	I have understood
Set and props	Any props you use must be significant and vital to the drama. Do not clutter your stage with props unless they are needed to sign meaning to an audience. The same can be said of your set. Often very simplistic sets can be as effective as elaborate ones. Using rostra to create levels and different spaces and focused lighting, that draw the audience's attention to specific areas of the stage, will be enough.			

Think tank

There are many other elements that make up the mediums of drama. We will focus more on them in the section of the book that explores Unit 3. Other mediums of drama include masks and make-up, sound and lighting, all of which you can find further details about in the design skills resource pack on this book's product page (www.rhinegold.co.uk).

Useful websites might include:

- An excellent resource about all aspects of theatre, which includes interviews with designers about their role: www.getintotheatre.org
- The Royal National Theatre has an excellent 'Discover' section that includes a virtual tour of theatre spaces and interviews with theatre practitioners, including theatre designers: www.nationaltheatre.org.uk. Follow the Discover link and then the Making Theatre link.
- Another excellent educational website that focuses on specific productions and has interviews with all the practitioners who have worked on them can be found at: www.stagework.org

You should be trying to use all the elements together. A good piece of drama needs all these elements working together. When you read a script or watch a live performance you should also look to see where these elements are being employed. Playwrights use these techniques to engage a live audience.

THE ELEMENTS OF DRAMA

Below are some examples of the drama elements. The exam board says that you must recognise these elements and understand how they assist and clarify the creation of drama.

Over the next few pages we look at some of the drama elements. Page 15 of the Edexcel GCSE specification will show you the full list. It is important to remember that you do not have to use all of the elements; it is up to you to choose and focus on specific elements depending on the work you are looking at.

Element	Definition	I have read	I have used	I have understood
Action/plot/content	These are the unfolding events of a story. You need to think about what events make up the content of your drama. When you plot the action you see the main narrative or story. The story of the play is simply the chain of events. Plot refers to the way the story unfolds and how all the events link together. Actions are what the character does in the play; these might be physical or psychological.			

Think tank

When we discuss plot we also have to reflect upon subtext, which is the secondary plot or storyline. When you are creating characters or discussing and analysing characters, subtext refers to the idea that there is meaning underneath the surface of what is being said or done. The use of subtext creates tension which in turn creates drama.

Element	Definition	I have read	I have used	I have understood
Climax/anti-climax	A narrative climax is the moment in the play when all the key ideas and strands of the narrative are brought together and everything is resolved. Often we feel the tension building towards a climatic point, and sometimes playwrights deliberately trick an audience into expecting something big to happen and then nothing does. This is an anti-climax.			

Think tank

An anti-climax is a good theatre technique if you are in control of its use. Good playwriting involves employing anti-climax, where you build your audience up to expect a climax and then do not give it to them. If you are not in control of it, and your play is anti-climactic, this means that it feels incomplete and can result in a disappointing or unsatisfying ending for your audience.

Strategy	Definition	I have read	I have used	I have understood
Rhythm and pace	Pace is the speed at which a scene, action in a scene or the whole play takes place. As an actor you must think about controlling the pace of your speeches. Rhythm is the pattern of sounds and movement in a speech or scene.			

Strategy	Definition	I have read	I have used	I have understood
Characterisation	The character is the person that the actor wishes to portray to an audience. The character will have a role within the piece. Character usually refers to an actual person. Characterisation is the way an actor decides to use his voice and body to represent the character they are portraying.			

Think tank

The antagonist in the play is the character who is in some kind of conflict with the main character or the protagonist in a play. In some plays it is difficult to decide who the antagonist and protagonist are, as you may find that the roles change throughout the play.

STYLES AND GENRES OF THEATRE

Developing your thinking

Why not use the internet to investigate plays and playwrights that match the genres, forms and styles below? This will broaden your knowledge of plays and playwrights and you will be able to reference them in your documentary response and class discussions.

When you create your drama in class and for Unit 3, you will need to think about what **genre, style or form, and conventions** you would like to use.

Genre reflects the content of your drama. Look at the spider diagram below and see what genres you are confident working within and ones that you may need to research further to clarify your understanding.

Form/style reflects the way your drama will look on the stage. Look at the spider diagram below and see which styles you are most confident working with and identify those that are new or less familiar and research them further to clarify your understanding.

Conventions are the drama elements and mediums that you will use to communicate the meaning of your performance to an audience. Look at the glossary on page xx to identify which conventions you are more confident in using and those that you may wish to research further to clarify your understanding

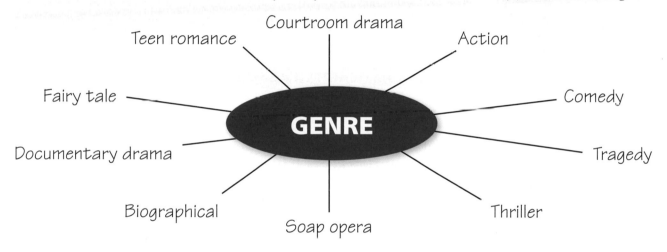

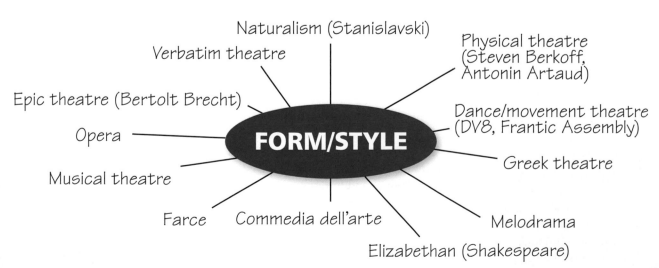

ANTONIN ARTAUD (1896-1948)

A **practitioner** is someone who is working practically in a particular field. A medical practitioner is someone who works practically in the field of medicine; a theatre practitioner is someone who works practically in the field of theatre. While you are working on this course, you are a theatre practitioner.

You should use the information on theatre practitioners as a starting point to the course and as a point of reference as you progress through your GCSE. You will not be examined directly on this information, but you should understand their influences on drama today, and you should experiment with their ideas practically.

Think tank

Artaud's vision for a radical new theatre has inspired many experimental companies since his death. It is an exciting process to apply some of Artaud's thinking and practice to your performance work. Artaud did not leave behind a whole shelf of plays or a series of exercises for actors to study; instead, Artaud left behind his visions for the theatre in a collection of essays under the title *The Theatre and Its Double*. Artaud was looking for performances in theatre that would assault the senses and lead to thought, creating an emotional rather than an intellectual theatre. Artaud's techniques, when applied, produce theatre that is bold, dynamic and 'in yer face'. It would be very difficult to use all of Artaud's ideas but, when applied, by putting some of his ideas into your performance work, you will be producing theatre that is dynamic, takes risks and is experimental.

WHAT WAS HE REACTING AGAINST?

Artaud, like Stanislavski, was reacting against the popular form of theatre that was prevalent as he was growing up. The accepted form of performance was declamatory, stilted and almost mechanical – there was no attempt to find the truth in a character and physical movements were almost stiff and unnatural. Both Artaud and Stanislavski wanted to bring some truth to the stage and strip away all that was superficial about the theatre, but these two practitioners went about this in very different ways.

ARTAUD'S LIFE

Artaud was born in France in 1896. By 1924, Artaud had become a poet, artist and a member of the Surrealist movement. He and his fellow Surrealists shared a vision of theatre as a place of free thinking, of emotional discovery and anarchy.

In 1926–1928, Artaud ran the Alfred Jarry Theatre. During this time he began to write his most famous theatrical work *Theatre of Cruelty*. In the early 1930s, Artaud watched a performance of Balinese dancers which blew him away and helped form his passionate beliefs for theatre. The Balinese dancers wore colourful masks and extravagant make-up; their performance was almost wordless – non-linguistic – as they acted out an old Hindu legend using movement and hand-gestures in a stylised way. The dancers were accompanied by percussion sounds produced by a gamelan. Artaud was struck by the magical quality of this work that broke actor/audience boundaries and appealed to the subconscious. Artaud wanted to devise drama that had the same effect on his audience as this dance had had on him.

Surrealism is a movement in art that seeks to express, talk about and show what is going on in the subconscious mind.

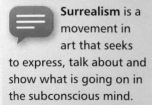

GETTY

GETTY

GETTY

A limited edition of *The Theatre and its Double* was published in 1937. From then onwards, Artaud spent many years in mental hospitals.

Towards the end of his life time, Artaud witnessed the rise of the Nazi party and he often said that society had become an evil boil that needed to be lanced by using his theatrical techniques. In January 1948, Artaud was diagnosed with cancer and died on 4 March 1948, allegedly sitting at the end of his bed holding his shoe.

TOTAL THEATRE

Total theatre is a style of modern theatre that has been developed from Artaud's ideas. Total theatre combines every theatrical element to create an assault on the audience's senses. The term 'Theatre of Cruelty' is associated with Artaud; it relates to a theatre of extremes, theatre that produces a totally sensory experience for the audience.

Overleaf are some of Artaud's thoughts and ideas from the *Theatre and its Double*; in the right-hand column are some suggested ways of experimenting with these ideas in your own dramas.

> ### Think tank
>
> Artaud says that the plague is a metaphor for theatre. The plague attacks all parts of the body and then attacks the heart of society. It has the ability to disrupt order, and this is how Artaud wanted to affect his audience. Think about the theatre you are making. Does it attack the senses in the body and raise questions about society? Is that what you want from your theatre?

The **actor/audience boundary** is the division between the audience and the stage action and the actors. If there are clear areas for the stage action, and the audience are sitting in front in their own space watching the action, then we have a rigid actor/audience boundary. If the stage action is happening all around the audience, where the actors may actually touch the audience and speak directly to them, then the actor/audience boundary has been broken, which is not necessarily a bad thing.

The **double** refers to theatre being the double of life and life being the double of true theatre. The double is also the inner feelings of a person that should be released in performance. The secret self that is usually contained and hidden away, but that should be freed. The double could also be those thoughts that we keep hidden inside of us because in polite society it is wrong to say the thoughts that are inside our minds.

Facts/techniques from Artaud's work	Thinking questions for your own practical work
Artaud believed that the **stage building** should be a big empty space, and that the action should happen all around the building. Artaud wanted to break the **actor/audience boundary** for 'the show' (this is what Artaud called his performances). The audience were to sit on swivel chairs in the centre of the space and the stage action was to take place all around them. The actors would invade the audience.	■ How can you lay out the seats for your audience so you break the actor/audience boundary? ■ Will you touch the audience or maybe talk to them? ■ How will you actually involve your audience in your performance? ■ Will you give the audience a role in your piece or will you give them an object as they enter your show?
Artaud focused on **sounds rather than words**. Screams were extremely important to him, as an actor was working to uncover raw emotions. Recorded sounds were often played at very high volume to assault the senses of his audience. Artaud also considered musical instruments to be very important to his shows; they not only create a feeling of ritual in the performance, but also created mood and atmosphere.	■ Are there emotions you can create on stage through making sounds rather than by saying words? ■ Are there any sections in your text that you can add soundscapes to to paint a picture in the audience's mind and to create mood and atmosphere? ■ Can you play sound effects or music at very high volume to assault your audience's senses? ■ Can screams be put into your production to express tormented inner emotions?
Artaud imagined that **lighting** should again attack the senses of his audience. The audience would be blinded by lights; lights would move around the space and would affect the audience on a subconscious level. These remained visions for Artuud as the technology did not exist or was limited at the time. For a better image of what Artaud wanted, imagine a rock concert or big arena gig and how they use lighting effects. This is what Artaud wanted for his shows.	■ Do you have access to lasers, strobes and moving lights for your drama work? How could you use these lighting effects to affect your audience and make them uncomfortable? ■ You may need to keep your lighting simple but still think about torches shining in the audience's face, or using overhead projectors facing the audience to blind them or turned around to flood the acting space with light.
Masks and make-up were used by Artaud to add a dream-like quality to his shows and to move them away from realism. Elaborate masks will encourage performers to find ways of expressing emotions physically and shocking bold make-up could challenge and disturb the audience.	■ Could your characters have bold and brash make-up; maybe white faces, black lipstick and blacked-out eyes? ■ How can you shock and disturb your audience through masks and make-up?
Artaud talked of actors **releasing the double**, revealing the truth behind simple actions, and showing what was really going on underneath realistic, naturalistic performances. Artaud believed his actors should be trained athletes who are able to push themselves beyond their own comfort zones and who could uncover raw and real emotion in performance.	■ Can you reveal the truth in your performance? One exercise that is often used is to naturalistically show a person on stage smoking, but then to reveal the double by focusing on the body and showing the audience what is happening inside, how the lungs are being damaged, and how the tar is clinging to the airways. The actor shows this to the audience through physical gestures and abstract sounds.

Think tank

Artaud's techniques are exciting and dynamic. Using these techniques requires you to be brave and to take some risks on stage. You may not be comfortable doing this at first but, if you keep working at it, through experimentation you can improve the standard and depth of your own performance work.

KONSTANTIN STANISLAVSKI (1863 – 1938)

Photograph from the archive of the Stanislavski Centre Rose Bruford College

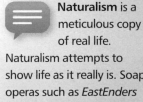

Stanislavski in Chekhov's *Uncle Vanya*

STANISLAVSKI CENTRE ROSE BRUFORD COLLEGE

Think tank

Stanislavski is often considered the father of modern Western theatre and actor training. He has had a huge influence on modern theatre practice. Stanislavski was reacting against the same style of 'mechanical acting' as Artaud, but Stanislavski tried to encourage an illusion of truth and reality in his work. He required that his actors became the characters they were playing by stepping into their shoes. Stanislavski was an actor and then a director, directing productions of Chekhov's major works. He left behind many books about his method of actor training called 'the system'. Stanislavski works within the naturalistic genre. As an actor you will probably have used some of Stanislavski's techniques without even realising it.

STANISLAVSKI'S LIFE

Stanislavksi was born in Russia in 1863 into a rich Russian family. He worked for a time as an actor, and in 1885 went to train at the Moscow Theatre School. He left three weeks later because he thought the training he was receiving there was poor. Instead Stanislavski set about watching other successful actors work, actors who had a real presence on stage, and worked to find a way of recreating their success in his own performances.

Naturalism is a meticulous copy of real life. Naturalism attempts to show life as it really is. Soap operas such as *EastEnders* work within the naturalistic genre. It is the dominant form on television today.

In 1897 Stanislavski co-founded the Moscow Arts Theatre and directed productions there between 1898 and 1904. Here Stanislavski began to develop a clear set of ideals rooted in Naturalism. This was a direct response to his disaffection with the style of brash, loud, gestural and declamatory acting that was common at the time in other theatres.

Stanislavski worked intensively with his actors to try to get them to portray the real emotional life of a character on stage. Their performances had to be detailed and truthful. He asked actors to explore characters both from the inside out and the outside in.

Stanislavski (sat on table) in Gorky's *The Lower Depths*

STANISLAVSKI CENTRE ROSE BRUFORD COLLEGE

In 1906 Stanislavksi went to Finland to begin work on the manual for his system of actor training. His system is extremely well documented and he eventually produced three books as a guide: *An Actor Prepares; Building a Character;* and *Creating a Role*.

Stanislavski died in 1938, but his techniques are still used to this day as tools that you can use during the rehearsal process when preparing to play a character. Many directors employ Stanislavski's techniques during rehearsals, and many drama schools in this country use elements of the system. Method actors in America, including Daniel Day Lewis, Tom Cruise and Dustin Hoffman, are trained using Strasberg's method, who developed Stanislavski's system into method acting, and again this is a dominant form of actor training and actor preparation in America.

Stanislavski would work to create a boundary between the actor and the audience. Naturalistic plays work best on a proscenium-arch stage, where there is a clear divide between audience and stage action. The audience sit outside the invisible fourth wall and spy in on people's lives as they are taking place. It is like watching an experiment with mice in a cage. The playwright puts the characters in social situations and the audience watches to witness the results.

> An important word here is **analogous** – an adjective that means similar in certain respects. As actors we should be looking for analogous emotions when we are playing a character. We need to find a real emotion in ourselves that is as similar as possible to the emotion the character is feeling in the play.

PRACTICAL APPLICATION

Overleaf are some of Stanislavski's thoughts and ideas from his system; in the right-hand column are some suggested ways of experimenting with these ideas in your own drama and during rehearsals and character preparation.

Think tank

Stanislavksi's techniques are very useful when you are rehearsing and thinking about characters for your performances. Even if your drama is abstract and non-naturalistic, it is important that you have a sense of character on stage and that you have developed your thinking about that character. Try not just to play the character's friends or the influences on the character – try and develop a fully rounded three-dimensional character for yourself on stage.

Facts/techniques from Stanislavski's work	Thinking questions for your own practical work
A key element of the system is **given circumstances**. These are the story, the facts in the play, the names, the setting/the location, in fact everything that that playwright tells you. As actors you are basing your character on the information the playwright has given you. Stanislavski encourages his actors to ask the characters the basic questions: who, what, where, when, and why? The answer to these questions goes to make up a character study for the actor.	For your Unit 2, or if you are using a script for Unit 3, character draw up a character study. Ask yourself all the key questions: ■ Who am I? ■ What do I want? ■ Where am I now? ■ Where am I from? ■ In what time period do I exist? ■ What do I want? ■ Why do I want it?
Stanislavski wanted the actor to use their own thoughts, emotions and memories to play a character. He used the term **Magic If** – the actor must ask himself the question: 'If I were this character how would I feel? What would I do if I were in this situation?'	Apply the Magic If questions to the characters you are playing in your practical work. If you have been in a situation that made you feel an emotion that is like your character's, then try to remember what you did and how you acted and use that information when you play the character.

Stanislavski would do a lot of work with the actual script before he got his actors up on the stage. He would divide the text into short sections with a title for each section. This is called **units and objectives.** Simply, a unit finishes when something on stage changes – a thought or maybe an action. Units can be different lengths. Each character is given an objective in the unit that tells us what they want. It might be 'to control my feelings' or 'to be alone' or 'to tell my dad what I am thinking'.

Try to take a short piece of script and divide it into units. A unit could be one line or a few speeches. When you have decided where the unit finishes, draw a line across the page. Then look at one character and ask yourself the simple question: what do they want to do right now? The answer to this becomes their objective for that unit.

Emotional memory was another element of the system, although it became the key element in the method. This exercise asks you as an actor to think of a time what you felt an emotion that is the same as the emotion the character is feeling. If you use that memory in your performance, then Stanislavski believes you are adding truthfulness to your character. When we talk about emotional truth we also have to think about **inners** and **outers**. Outers are the emotions we show to and share with the world. Inners are emotions we keep hidden and choose not to share with or show to anyone.

Using your own memory bank to portray an emotional truth on stage is a very personal experience. It is probably something you will work on privately at home and then bring the results to your rehearsals. Essentially you are trying to remember how you felt and more importantly what you did when you felt that emotion. You then bring those physical actions and give them to your character.

A **Marxist** is an individual who follows the writing of German socialist writer, Karl Marx. A socialist believes that resources and industry should be owned by the state and run for the good of the people rather than run to make money.

BERTOLT BRECHT (1898-1956)

Think tank

You will be using many of Brecht's performance ideas in the way that you work without even realising it. Brecht was a playwright and a director but he always wrote about theatre and developed many theories for performance. Brecht is a political playwright, and it was his politics that guided his thoughts about theatre. Since Brecht, many theatre practitioners have used theatre to show their thoughts and feelings about political issues. Brecht wanted to make his audience think about why characters in plays make the decisions they make. Brecht was a left-wing Marxist playwright.

BRECHT'S LIFE

Brecht was born into a middle-class family in Germany in 1898. He studied medicine and served in an army hospital during World War I. Brecht was sickened by the horrors he witnessed during the war and developed anti-war sentiments.

Brecht began to write plays and speak out against the Nazi party. He built up a large catalogue of plays during this time including *Drums in the Night*, *Baal*, and *In Jungle of the Cities*. In 1933 he was forced to go into exile from the Nazi party and he firstly fled to Switzerland and then Denmark, before eventually travelling

GETTY

GETTY

Brecht was reacting against the form and content of plays that followed the work of Stanislavski, plays that were concerned with empathy, emotions and feeling. Brecht wanted theatre that was concerned with distance, thinking and reason.

to America where he continued to work as a playwright and a director. Back in Germany, his books and plays were banned by the Nazi party and his texts were burned. In 1949 Brecht returned to a divided Germany where he set up his own theatre company, The Berliner Ensemble. The Berliner Ensemble staged many of Brecht's greatest plays and it was while he was with the ensemble that he developed many of his theories for performance. Here he developed **epic theatre** – a style of theatre that places political messages before the exploration and development of character.

Brecht did not want audiences to become emotionally involved with a performance on stage; instead he wanted them to think about stage action and how they might change situations presented in the play. He called this *Verfremdung*, a German word which literally means 'to make strange'. The idea was that the audience would stand back from the action, not to feel but to think about what they had seen.

Brecht died in 1956 and popular myth has is that he was buried in a steel coffin so his body would not decompose in the ground, because he didn't in any way want to return to a society which he saw as essentially unequal and unfair.

PRACTICAL APPLICATION

Overleaf are some of Brecht's thoughts and ideas from his writing about *Verfremdung* and epic theatre. In the right-hand column are some suggested ways of experimenting with these ideas in your own drama, during rehearsals and character preparation.

Think tank

All Brecht's techniques ask his audience and actors to take a step away from the characters they are playing or watching and to question them. Why are they in the situations they are in? What can we do to change the situation these characters find themselves in? You may not use Brechtian techniques for the political reasons Brecht intended but, nevertheless, they are useful techniques in rehearsal and performance.

You will all soon be old enough to vote in the UK and have a say in who runs this country. How much do you know about politics? Do you know what the terms left-wing and right-wing actually mean? Why do we not have many lessons in school about politics? Lay out two pieces of paper at either end of your drama classroom, one saying left-wing and one saying right-wing. Ask your teacher to simply explain the differences. Once you understand the difference, stand on the line in the position you think the following ideas go: the National Health Service; private education; the idea of the Labour Party; the idea of the Conservative Party. It is useful to have a developed understanding of these terms when you are studying Brecht.

Facts/techniques from Brecht's work	Thinking questions for your own practical work
Brecht wanted to use **banners and placards** at the side of the stage to announce facts to the audience. In this way you can keep your set simply and represent a place rather than try to recreate the place on stage.	You could use placards at the start of a scene to tell the audience where the scene is set, or what time period it is set in. You might introduce your characters at the start of a performance with a placard telling the audience their name and their internal thoughts.
In a Brechtian production the actors would **multi-role**; in this way maybe two or three actors would play one character. This would stop the audience getting too attached to the character as they would be performed by different actors.	If you use multi-role in your performance work you need to let the audience know when you are playing a character. Maybe you have a simple piece of clothing that is passed to you as you take on that character. Maybe you are all dressed the same when you become the character. Maybe different actors could show different sides of the same character.
Brecht wanted to break the **actor/audience boundary** and wanted his actors to use direct address when they break the fourth wall and talk directly to the audience in and out of role.	You could try using direct address at the start of your performance to tell the audience what they are going to watch. You could try stopping the stage action at one point in your piece and marking the moment by stepping out of role and telling the audience what you personally feel about what is happening on stage.
Breaking the illusion: Brecht wanted to break the illusion of theatre and tell the audience they were not watching real life up on stage to remind them they were just watching a performance. There were many ways to distance the audience and to break the illusion: simple sets that were representational rather than trying to recreate real life; scene changes that happened in front of the audience; lighting that could be seen and wasn't hidden away to create illusion.	As your performance starts, you could already be sitting on stage, maybe on chairs at the side or along the back. You don't have to disappear off stage. Maybe the audience could see you warming up or rehearsing before the performance begins. You could keep your set very simple, a chair to represent a throne, a wooden block could become a car, a wall or a kitchen table. Do you really need to make everything on stage look realistic?

Maybe you could have a CD player on stage and when you need music you could just walk over to it and switch it on in view of the audience. The same could happen with your lighting-control board. Does it have to be hidden away or could the audience see the person who is operating it? |
| **Epic structure**: Brecht's plays followed the epic structure in which lots of different scenes were presented rather than just Act 1 and Act 2. Between scenes, Brecht said you could jump forward days or weeks or years, or alternatively you could jump back in time. The scenes do not have to follow on from one another in time order. | Have you seen the musical of *Blood Brothers*? At the start of the show you see the final scene; this is part of the epic structure. The play itself covers many years. This is not something a true naturalistic play can do, but you can do this if you are working in the epic structure. When you come to put a performance together does it have to go in time order or could you show the last scene first? Then the audience knows what will happen and can concentrate on *why* it happens. |
| **Spaß** (pronounced Spasz) is the German word for fun. Brecht would introduce moments of Spaß into his plays for a number of reasons. It might be to lighten the mood, to allow us time to think about what we have seen, or it may be employed to mock certain characters. | Think about the use of comedy in your performances. You might want to mock a certain character and make them look silly because you disagree with what they are doing and saying. It might make a moment of tragedy more shocking if you are laughing at the characters one minute and then are shocked by what you see them doing the next. |

There are many techniques contained in pages 20 – 27 from different practitioners. Have you seen any of these techniques used in productions you have seen? Do you regularly use any of these techniques in your own drama work? Try and use different practitioner's techniques when you make up your own drama. Once you have used a technique, look back over these eight pages and see which practitioner the technique comes from. It is acceptable to use a technique for a different reason to the original practitioner, but what is important is that you know what the original practitioner was trying to achieve with each of their techniques. A last question to think about is why are these practitioners from the past all men?

THEATRE LAYOUTS

What follows is information on different layouts. It is included to spark new ideas and to suggest ways in which you can perform to your audience in your dramas. When you share your drama with your class during Units 1 and 2, think about which theatre layout will best serve your drama. When you come to create your pieces of theatre for Unit 3, experiment with different layouts for your audience.

A drama performance has three main elements; it has actors, an audience and it takes place in a given space. The layout of the performance space must be considered, as different layouts have their own advantages and disadvantages. It is easy to move your audience in your classroom to create different performance spaces, and you should consider what performance layout is best for each scene you present to an audience. Think about the actor/audience boundary. Do you want the audience to remain distant from your action as detached observers or do you want to include them directly in the action and therefore break the actor/audience boundary?

PROSCENIUM ARCH OR END ON

The Junction, Sunshine Coast, Australia

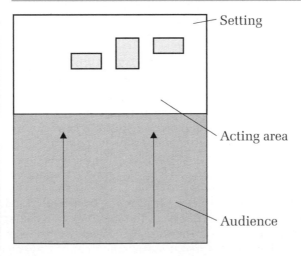

Setting

Acting area

Audience

This theatre layout is regarded as the most traditional form for theatres. In an end-on layout, the audience are placed straight in front of the acting area, which is a separate space, giving the audience the impression they are looking in on the action through a picture frame. The proscenium arch is the divide between the actors and the audience. It is sometimes referred to as the 'fourth wall'.

The box set is seen to have three walls: upstage, stage left and stage right, and the fourth wall is the invisible wall that divides the actor and the action from the audience. The identification of left and right on stage is always from the actor's point of view.

CHALLENGES

The divide between the action and the audience created by the fourth wall means your audience will not feel so involved in your stage action. It is a comfortable place sitting end-on, knowing there is a divide between actor and audience. This may mean the audience stays in their comfort zone. Is this what you want from your drama?

This theatre layout is often associated with naturalistic theatre and may not work so well for other performance genres.

Audiences are used to this theatre layout and could sit back comfortably and let the piece wash over them, rather than sitting on the edge of their seat, ready for things to happen, ready to listen, observe and think about the stage action.

IMPACT ON AUDIENCE

It is easy to create realistic settings and also to use the sides of the stage for surprise entrances and effects. Audiences are used to this theatre layout and feel comfortable and safe. In this layout there is a clear sense of them (actors) and us (audience).

Think tank

See the discussion of Stanislavski from pages 23 to 24 to read about a practitioner whose work is best suited to this theatre layout.

In this theatre layout, illusion can be created. We can create realistic settings and employ naturalistic acting styles. Done at its best, this style of performance can make the audience forget they are watching a play and may transport them to another world, presenting action over which the audience feels it has no control. The world presented on the stage is not the audience's world, but a make-believe world that exists behind the proscenium arch. Is this the type of theatre you want to create?

TRAVERSE

The Traverse Theatre, Edinburgh

© GAVIN HARDING

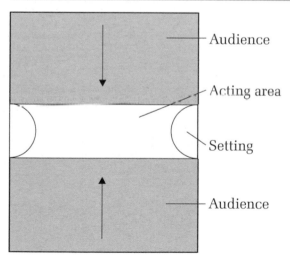

Audience

Acting area

Setting

Audience

There may be performances where you want your audience to be able to see each other. This will remind them that they are watching a play. This may also make the audience feel as if they are part of the action. If we believe that drama is about raising questions and asking an audience to think, then it may be necessary that the audience are reminded they are watching a play and that there are other people in the audience who are also part of this shared experience.

When a play is staged in traverse, the audience sit on either side of a corridor. This theatre layout is sometime referred to as 'theatre-in-the-corridor'; the acting area is the space in the middle of two blocks of seating. This type of layout brings the audience very close to the action and allows them to see the audience on the opposite side of the acting area. The layout means you cannot use big pieces of scenery in the middle acting area, but you could put larger pieces of set at either end of the corridor. Traverse layout gives the actor a close relationship with the audience. This layout breaks the actor/audience boundary.

CHALLENGES

This theatre layout limits the use of much scenery as anything placed in the central acting area will get in the way of the audience and may mean they can not see all the stage action as their sightlines will be blocked. The audience can only be a couple of rows deep to ensure all members can see the action, or the audience needs to be raked in tiers. The two end areas offer potential to place larger pieces of scenery, but they also create difficulties in relation to sightlines. They will have to look sideways over the heads of other audience members to see. This layout makes the blocking of action difficult. Wherever an actor is standing in the central area, he will be blocking a member of the audience's view of the action. A director will have to keep moving the characters around to ensure an audience's view is not blocked for too long.

IMPACT ON AUDIENCE

Setting needs to be created through words (linguistics). This allows the actor to paint vivid and elaborate sets in the audience's minds. One member of the audience is always able to see another audience member. We are reminded that we are watching a play with other people – they are sharing the experience – and we are also able to see how other people are reacting to the action on stage. This is a simple theatre layout to set up in a classroom.

IN THE ROUND

Theatre in the Round Players, Inc., Minneapolis, Minnesota

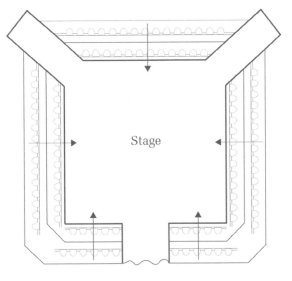
Stage

For some performances you may want to create a very intimate atmosphere where the audience almost feel part of the action themselves. You may wish to explore action that needs to be small, under projected and subtle. Your choice and organisation of your performance space will affect the way your audience responds to your performance.

The in-the-round type of layout refers to the fact that the audience surround the acting area, which does not have to be round exactly. A good example of the layout is a boxing ring, surrounded by tiered seating for the audience on four sides. Most studio theatres can be configured in this way.

CHALLENGES

The Allen Theatre arena stage at ACT – A Contemporary Theatre, Seattle, Washington

© MICHAEL ALLEN

Like the traverse theatre layout, it is difficult to have large pieces of set in this layout as they will block the audience's view of the stage action. Blocking is a problem in this layout. In most positions in the space an actor will have his back to an audience member and will be blocking the action. The actor needs to ensure they share their performance with all four sides of audience.

The intimate layout needs to be reflected in a smaller intimate style of acting, being subtle and controlled.

Scene changes can not be hidden from the audience and therefore need to be integrated into your stage action.

IMPACT ON AUDIENCE

Royal Exchange Theatre, Manchester

The actor/audience boundary is broken and there is a real sense of sharing the action. The intimacy creates a more interesting experience for the audience as they feel part of what is happening on stage. The actors and, therefore, the stage action are very close to audience members in this layout.

Actors can achieve a very naturalistic style of acting as the audience are so close; there is no need to project your performance to ensure everyone can see it.

Think tank

You could also think about using the space behind the audience. How could you use this to further break down actor/audience boundary? Your audience will be feeling exposed; could you play on this to create tension, fear, or suspense in your audience? Look at discussions of Artaud's techniques on pages 20 to 22.

PROMENADE AND SITE SPECIFIC

Promenade theatre, The Walking Theatre Company

Does theatre have to take place in a conventional theatre building? In recent years, there have been productions that have taken their theatre outside the walls of a building – on streets, in parks, car parks, underground, in cars, or on buses. The work of the theatre company Shunt takes place in underground passages below ground, under railway arches. Any space can become a performance space as long as you have three elements: actors, audience and space. You may walk your audience between different settings or you may create a piece of theatre to suit a particular space.

This type of layout refers to the fact that the audience moves around – or promenades – to see what is being presented. The audience don't usually sit down and are allowed to walk wherever they wish to view the stage action. You could stage a promenade piece in a theatre, as the Royal National Theatre did for its promenade production of the *Mystery Cycle*, or you could stage one in a building not usually used for theatre, or even outside. A site-specific performance is a performance that is devised to suit a particular place. This could be an old house, a park, a forest or a changing room in your school. It might be interesting to move around your school to find interesting and exciting spaces where your dramas could take place.

CHALLENGES

Grid Iron's production of
The Devil's Larder, staged in
Debenham's, Edinburgh as part
of Traverse Festival 2005

Depending on the size of the space you are performing, you may have to limit your audience to fit the space. You have to remember the audience may not behave as you want them to. They may not move around and typically they will find a place to sit down or perch and remain there for the performance. You have to think about how you will move the audience from location to location and build this into the stage action. If you are performing outside there are obviously influences that may be out of your control, such as noise from trains and passing cars, and people walking past who are not part of the audience. Lighting and sound are difficult for promenade and site-specific productions; remember it is more difficult to project vocally outside. There are also a lot of health and safety issues that need to be considered.

IMPACT ON AUDIENCE

This style of performance can be very exciting for an audience. It may be a form of performance that they have never experienced before. It engages the audience and brings them right into the centre of your performance; they almost become part of the action and you treat them as if they are playing a role in the drama. They might become mourners at a funeral, or patients in a waiting room. Think about completely breaking down the actor/audience boundary.

PRACTICAL EXPLORATION OF AN EXTRACT FROM FICTION OR NON-FICTION

The book *Dark Heart: the Shocking Truth about Hidden Britain* by Nick Davies (Chatto and Windus 1997) is a rich source of material for drama. In 2008 alone, the National Theatre of Scotland used the text as a starting point for their production *365*. Frantic Assembly also used the text to help define the context for their production of Shakespeare's *Othello*.

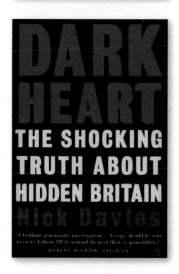

The adjacent extract is from *Dark Heart* by Nick Davies. As you read the story, use a highlighter to mark text that shocks you, provokes thought or moves you. This will then feed into your work on your documentary response.

Remember that in this unit you will use both explorative strategies and drama mediums to explore themes, topics and issues that have been decided by your teacher. Through using drama mediums and strategies you will devise your own drama.

Your teacher will offer a variety of stimuli that you will work on in class. These will be based on themes, topics or issues and you will make connections between them.

Unit 1 focuses more on the way you create your drama together rather than the final performance. You will be continually assessed in class by your teacher. You will take notes after each session to help form your final written documentary response of 2,000 words; this will be completed in class time under supervision.

> **Extract from *Dark Heart: Hidden Britain* (Chatto and Windus 1997) by Nick Davies, abridged from pages 148-151**
>
> The school doors have just opened for the day, and the children are arriving from every corner of the estate: out of the tower blocks with the spray-paint on the walls; past the empty houses with their windows all 'tinned up' against the thieves; down the road where the young woman was murdered; round the corner where the old Alsatian dog shouts; and into the playground. Just about nobody arrives by car. Outside the doors, it is chaos. A boy shows off the ear-stud he has been given for his birthday. A girl falls off the school wall and takes a cuff across the shoulder from her mother. Somewhere, a car alarm starts screaming. A mother in a dirty tracksuit shouts 'Stop it now!' at the baby in her buggy. The boy loses his ear-stud and starts to scream. Two small boys and a girl scavenge among the rubbish that the wind has collected. Then the parents start to drift away, the school doors close, and something rather strange begins to happen.
>
> This primary school survives in a state of siege. The poverty invades the school. You can see it in the fabric of the building, which has bars on its windows and a spiked fence around its grounds: even so, joy-riders career around the playing fields at night and intruders routinely rob the place at weekends, leaving behind them a trail of broken windows, graffiti and syringes …
>
> And yet the school fights back …
>
> Looking at the children now, you can see only the tiniest hints of their lives outside. A couple of them are heaving with fatigue. Others have shabby clothes and broken shoes and there is something oddly adult about some of them: the eleven-year-old girl with her tight black mini-skirt and her T-shirt that says she's '100% babe'; the little boys with men's faces …

There are other types of stimuli that you might look at during your GCSE drama study. On page 37 the stimuli is a collection of photographs. Pages 39–41 offers song lyrics as a starting point. Page 42 uses a very short extract of a drama text and page 48 offers you a poem as a starting point. Other stimuli you might be offered include extracts from films, from newspapers and significant objects (artefacts).

There is a boy who mutilates himself, digging into his arms with any tool he can find, acting out some unnamed horror at home. Sometimes the clues to the damage are obvious, like the children who have been acting out hardcore pornography in the playground, copying videos they have seen at home. Sometimes the clues are harder to see: the boy who was suddenly sullen because, in the background, his elder brother had been jailed for five years …

There are children here who will survive, perhaps because their families have managed to resist the stresses of life on the estate, perhaps because the school itself will offer a way out. But those are the exceptions …

These children have no dreams. The nearest they have to role models are junk heroes from pulp fiction … Seeds of hope are allowed to grow for about six hours and then the school has to uproot them and send the children home – home where a two-year-old sister fell out of an upstairs window the other week because no-one was looking after her … These children have no hope. They live in a state of despair.

Think tank

Your teacher may give you a piece of text as a starting point. Read it through once and then on your second reading have a highlighter pen to hand. Highlight any interesting sections, any sections that describe characters, and any sections that describe places and locations. You may wish to colour code these annotations. Close your eyes. What do you see in your mind's eye when you reflect on the piece of text from *Dark Heart: Hidden Britain* on page 33? You need to be able to discuss what the starting point meant to you and how you developed ideas from it using dramatic techniques.

Developing your thinking

The book *Dark Heart: Hidden Britain* is published by Chatto and Windus and contains essays by Nick Davies, an investigative journalist. Reading the book will give you many ideas and starting points for explorative drama; it will also give you lots of ideas for devised work in Unit 3. An internet search for Nick Davies may also throw up some interesting potential articles.

THEMES

In the following sections of this guide, we will extend your thinking about the themes contained within the stimulus material.

Another way of using this rubric is:

My heart tells me …

My head tells me …

My eyes tell me …

My ears tell me …

Developing your thinking

Can you find an extract from a film, DVD or a recording from a television programme that you could bring in that you think shows the environment the young people described in the *Dark Heart: Hidden Britain* extract live in?

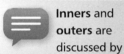

Inners and **outers** are discussed by Stanislavski. Revise Stanislavski and the discussion about inner and outer emotions on pages 23 to 24.

Your teacher may call a **still image** by another name. You may be familiar with **tableaux**. Another term used to describe this technique is **depiction**. A depiction is a frozen moment of action that clearly shows something happening. The depiction holds energy; bodies should be tense not lazy. You would not be able to move any part of a person who is in a dynamic depiction.

An immediate way to respond to a starting point is to use a framework for your thinking (a rubric). Use the following rubric to respond to the extract on page 33. Your teacher may use this rubric to ask you to respond to any given starting point.

> This starting point made me feel …
>
> This starting point made me think …
>
> This starting point made me see …
>
> This starting point made me hear …

Ensure you record your answers in your notebook. You should always record what you did in drama sessions and your thoughts and feelings about the session. Also note down any questions the work might raise for you.

? Thinking questions

1. What do these children need from school?
2. What is school offering them?
3. Is our education system appropriate for these students?

DRAMA STRATEGIES

In these sections we will look at which strategies you might decide to use. The list of drama strategies can be found on page 12.

When you are given a starting point in drama, your first decision must be what explorative strategies will be best for exploring and thinking about this starting point.

Select one of the children mentioned in the *Dark Heart* extract. Create a character profile around them. The most efficient way of creating a character profile is by using a **role on the wall**. Your teacher may ask you to draw the outline of a human figure on a large piece of paper in the shape of a gingerbread man. Details about your character are placed within the outline. You can then choose what to record on the outside. In this case you could identify all the particular pressures that are placed on that character or the influences that make that character who they are. Your teacher may ask you to record other facts about the character.

You might want to make a link with the character and one of the images on page 37.

Another way of exploring character is to use the strategy of still image and thought-tracking. Create a still image of a child standing outside the school gates. Thought track the child. When you thought track, you speak the thoughts that are in your character's head. This helps develop the role and gives everyone a chance to hear the thoughts of the characters in the drama.

Simply think what you are communicating to your audience; what you want to say to them and what you want them to feel. Think of the best strategies and drama mediums to communicate that meaning. In some cases your teacher may tell you what strategies and mediums they want you to use, but there is always room to try others out as well. This will help raise your marks.

You may work linguistically (with words as a focus) or non-linguistically (with as few words used as possible). The use of levels and space and height to communicate meaning is known as **proxemics**. Using correct drama key words will raise your marks in your documentary response.

You are now building up your explorative skills and reflective skills. You have focused on how to respond to a starting point, how to develop characters from a piece of text and then how to take the characters and, using the context of the text, use those characters in drama.

You could use thought-tracking within your performance as an extra technique. Maybe freeze the action and have a character come forward and face the audience, using the Brechtian technique of direct address to tell the audience what they are like and their thoughts on what is happening. See pages 25 to 27 for more information about Brecht.

Ensure you note down all the drama strategies that you have used and employed.

- Name and then describe the strategy
- Say why you used it
- Say what you learnt from using it.

COMMUNICATION

In these sections we will suggest ways of developing the work into performance for your class. As you prepare, you will start to choose which drama mediums you will use in your performance. The list of drama mediums can be found on page 14. Your teacher may tell you some drama mediums they want you to include, but to gain top marks you will need to think for yourself what other mediums you could employ. Don't forget you can include drama strategies in your performance work. As you become more confident with your drama, you will realise that top marks are achieved when you begin to employ strategies and mediums together to communicate meaning to an audience. For this starting point you could work in pairs to prepare an improvisation, marking the moment when the child says goodbye to the person who has brought them to school, before walking into the school gates.

 Things to remember

- The scene takes place outside the school gates in the street. There is a low-running wall running along the front of the school
- Work for significance of action. Try and find a moment of action that reveals the truth of the relationship rather than the public face they choose to show the world
- Try and work without words
- Think about the use of levels.

Remember to make a note of your scene in your notebook. Also make a note of your evaluation of other people's performance. Choose a member from your class who played the main role today. Write a short but clear account of their performance. Be sure to comment on:

- Their use of movement
- Their use of voice
- Their use of strategies
- The impact their performance had on the audience
- Any improvements you would suggest.

THEMES

▪ Love ▪ War ▪ Pain ▪ Journeying ▪ Despair ▪ Hope ▪ Destruction ▪ Power
▪ Poverty ▪ Corruption ▪ Religion ▪ Passion ▪ Worship ▪ Innocence.

? Thinking questions

1. Look at the image and write around it words that you think link to the picture.
2. When you look at the image what do you think is going on inside the head of the characters.
3. Looking closely at the background of the image, what other characters would you imagine being there? What would they be thinking, seeing, hearing and feeling?
4. Thinking about the world of the image, what sounds could you imagine happening?
5. If you had to title the image with something that encompasses the feelings it conveys, what would it be?
6. Think of the person that created the image; what was their intention for the audience?
7. What would have happened an hour before the image was captured?
8. What do you think happened an hour after this image was taken?

STRATEGIES

See Brechtian techniques on pages 25 to 27.

Begin by **recreating the image** that you see in the picture. Attempt to recreate the actions using an actor. If you can include basic props to represent the background it could help you understand the world for this character. **Thought track** the character in the image (maybe the characters that you imagined would be in the world of the picture). This can be said directly to the audience or you can develop your short piece of writing into a monologue. Find a space and sit alone imagining you are in role as a character from the image. Using a small A5 piece of paper, write a diary entry as if you are in their situation structured around the following five questions:

▪ What is their action (what are they doing)?
▪ What is their motivation (why are they doing it)?
▪ Who is your model (where have you seen this before)?
▪ What will you gain (what will you get out of it)?
▪ What is your stance (what is the world for you)?

This technique can help deepen your understanding of your role and character. Ensure that you use connectives in your answers to avoid one-word responses or simple sentences.

Choose one or more significant objects that you think could signify to an audience something about the character. These could be naturalistic (objects that they would really have like medals, diary or a key ring) or abstract (non-naturalistic), such as chains, red or black cloth. Using your writing in role, choose some powerful lines of text from your diary entry and try saying them directly to the audience (see Brechtian techniques from pages 25 to 27). To address the main themes that the pictures highlight, find some related facts and write them onto large placards that can be displayed in your performance.

COMMUNICATION

- Think about how you will demand your audience's attention.
- Where will you place yourself on the stage area?
- Where will you be in relation to other actors and what messages will that communicate to the audience?
- Where will you place the objects that you have chosen and how will you use them in your scenes?
- When will you use direct address to get your social or political message across to your audience?
- If you or someone in your group can sing, what song could you include?
- Wherever possible add **action**. Your play will be more like a radio play if you rely too much on text.
- Choral movement and choral speaking can be really powerful in performance; by choosing the most significant actions and most powerful lines of text you can create a dynamic piece of theatre.

DEVELOPING DRAMA FROM SONG LYRICS

Think tank

You can use song lyrics that you think link to the main themes of what you are studying in class. Make sure that you look carefully at how the songs link. Communicate those links clearly in your documentary response and in your class drama.

THEMES

Read the lyrics and, with a highlighter, select words that directly link to the images from the previous page. Circle any of the lyrics that are actions. These can be used when you need to communicate your ideas using drama conventions. As you listen to the music what images, colours, words, memories are conjured up for you? These songs are a narrow selection; think about songs you know that are relevant to your theme and include these in your class work. Look at who recorded the song originally and identify the intentions behind the song, this will open up a new area of themes and issues for you to use.

REM: *EVERYBODY HURTS*

When the day is long and the night, the night is yours alone,
When you're sure you've had enough of this life, well hang on.
Don't let yourself go, 'cause everybody cries and everybody
hurts sometimes.

Sometimes everything is wrong. Now it's time to sing along
When your day is night alone, (hold on, hold on).
If you feel like letting go, (hold on).
When you think you've had too much of this life, well hang on.

'Cause everybody hurts. Take comfort in your friends.
Everybody hurts. Don't throw your hand. Oh, no. Don't
throw your hand
If you feel like you're alone, no, no, no, you are not alone.

If you're on your own in this life, the days and nights are long,
When you think you've had too much of this life to hang on.

Well, everybody hurts sometimes,
Everybody cries. And everybody hurts sometimes
And everybody hurts sometimes. So, hold on, hold on
Hold on, hold on, hold on, hold on, hold on, hold on
Everybody hurts. You are not alone.

LEONARD COHEN: *HALLELUJAH*

Now I've heard there was a secret chord
That David played, and it pleased the Lord
But you don't really care for music, do you?
It goes like this
The fourth, the fifth
The minor fall, the major lift
The baffled king composing Hallelujah.
Hallelujah
Hallelujah
Hallelujah
Hallelujah

Your faith was strong but you needed proof
You saw her bathing on the roof
Her beauty and the moonlight overthrew you.
She tied you
To a kitchen chair
She broke your throne, and she cut your hair
And from your lips she drew the Hallelujah.

Baby I have been here before
I know this room, I've walked this floor
I used to live alone before I knew you.
I've seen your flag on the marble arch
Love is not a victory march
It's a cold and it's a broken Hallelujah.

Hallelujah, Hallelujah
Hallelujah, Hallelujah

There was a time you let me know
What's really going on below
But now you never show it to me, do you?
And remember when I moved in you
The holy dove was moving too
And every breath we drew was Hallelujah.
Hallelujah, Hallelujah
Hallelujah, Hallelujah

You say I took the name in vain
I don't even know the name
But if I did, well really, what's it to you?
There's a blaze of light
In every word
It doesn't matter which you heard
The holy or the broken Hallelujah.

Hallelujah, Hallelujah
Hallelujah, Hallelujah

I did my best, it wasn't much
I couldn't feel, so I tried to touch
I've told the truth, I didn't come to fool you.
And even though
It all went wrong
I'll stand before the Lord of Song
With nothing on my tongue but Hallelujah.

Hallelujah, Hallelujah
Hallelujah, Hallelujah
Hallelujah, Hallelujah
Hallelujah, Hallelujah
Hallelujah, Hallelujah
Hallelujah, Hallelujah
Hallelujah, Hallelujah
Hallelujah, Hallelujah
Hallelujah

DAMIEN RICE: *COLD WATER*

Cold, cold water surrounds me now
And all I've got is your hand
Lord, can you hear me now?
Lord, can you hear me now?
Lord, can you hear me now,
Or am I lost?

No one's daughter, allow me that
And I can't let go of your hand
Lord, can you hear me now?
Lord, can you hear me now?
Lord, can you hear me now?
Or am I lost?

Oooo, I love you
Don't you know I love you
And I always have
Hallelujah
Will you come with me?

Cold, cold water surrounds me now

And all I've got is your hand
Lord, can you hear me?
Lord, can you hear me now?
Lord, can you hear me?
Ahh ...

Am I lost with you?
Am I lost with you?
Am I lost with you?

Juxtaposition: try juxtaposing the music with a scene from your work. This means choosing a scene that may be serious in tone and deals with contentious issues while playing an upbeat song. It really is worth trying. You will capture a more unnerving and sinister atmosphere if you choose the song carefully. You will notice that the audience are bombarded with disturbing images while listening to an upbeat and usually happy song. This can increase the audience's sense of pathos and empathy for a situation.

STRATEGIES

Using the lyrics that you have circled, select one and create it as a still image. Taking one of the characters from the song lyrics and one of the locations, draw a picture or create a scene.

Add into your scene the thoughts of the characters; remember to say what you see, hear, think and feel. Using the song lyrics break the verses down and choose some of the lines and turn them into titles for your drama. These can be put onto placards or a PowerPoint presentation.

COMMUNICATION

Using the lyrics from your chosen song you can underscore your drama by playing the song. You can choose the most powerful words and chant them together as a whole group. Select the most significant words from your song and write them onto T-shirts, a white sheet, or large pieces of paper to communicate to your audience the importance of them. You may wish to break the song into sections and divide the parts between you and your peers

Think tank

How will you break the
actor/audience boundary?
Will you use real objects
that symbolise the
emotions you are trying
to communicate? See
Antonin Artaud's theories
on pages 20 to 22.

Think tank

Using lyrics from a song can be very powerful for an audience. You can sing them,
project or use them as spoken word. What is important is that you listen to the
lyrics and understand their connections. You must be careful not to make tenuous
links. There must be a strong connection that you have communicated to your
audience. Music can be used as an underscore to the scene, similar to how it is
employed in film, where the music supports the acting, or it can be used as an
integral part of a scene. If you find a song that is integral to the themes of the
piece of drama that you are creating, you may think about performing it live to
the audience.

DEVELOPING DRAMA FROM A SCRIPT EXTRACT

SCRIPT ANALYSIS

Here is an example of a short extract from a script. Look and see how the
candidate has evaluated and applied their understanding. The extract below from
Seeds of Survival shows a journalist studying a child's behaviour.

Seeds of Survival

*An alleyway. It is dark. The corner where two dirty walls meet. One wall is higher than the other. One has
a window from which a light shines onto the street below. To one side a dustbin sits, overflowing. A small
child's ball sits on the street. The street is not clean.*

*A child sits on a box on the street, leaning against the corner. They are staring up at the window from where
we hear voices.*

The child holds a small school bag. It is full, but shut. The voices stop, and the child looks away.

*The child kicks the ball and it rolls down the street towards the journalist. The voices start again. The child
looks up and smiles.*

The journalist smiles to himself and picks up the ball. The journalist walks towards the child.

Journalist: I think this is yours.

The child holds tightly onto their schoolbag

The child stares at the journalist.

The voices stop and the child looks back up to the window.

Journalist: Do you know them?

The child shakes their head.

Child: Don't know who they all are, and is what mine?

The child pulls the bag closer towards their body and holds on tightly.

STUDENT DEVELOPMENT WORK

This whole text provides an in-depth look at a simple scene where we see a child looking for comfort in a home that they do not belong to. The title *Seeds of Survival* itself suggests that this text is about how to survive. If we do not have the right seeds, such as a good education, then perhaps we will not survive. The ball could be seen to represent the innocence of the child and their hopes. The stage instruction for the child to sit on a box signifies their isolation and wish to be alone. The child stares up at the window for comfort; the child probably had a family like this once. The child's schoolbag represents the bond they have with their school and how important school is to this child. The child kicks the ball to show his anger and how he hates life. He also wants the journalist to react. The reason the child is so scared of the journalist is because they feel isolated and separate from society; they no longer trust anyone else but themselves.

THEMES

Read the extract and underline the words, characters and images that you think directly link to the lyrics, images and themes that you have been exploring. Highlight the significant actions in the script and, like a story board, you should give each section a title. From these titles you will be able to identify the main themes that the whole play deals with. When reading a script you will notice that each character has an individual motivation and journey. It is important that you read the character's journey and identify what their overall objectives are in the script.

To look for the character's objective in the scene you should ask the following questions:

- What does the character want?
- Have they achieved this by the end of the scene?

> Knowing the character's wants and desires at the beginning of the play will help you as an actor to understand the motivations beneath their actions.

This will give you a better understanding of what their objective is at the beginning of the scene. Be aware that some characters achieve what they want and some do not (see page 23 on Stavislavski). Choosing a section of the script, prepare the scene working for significance of action and movement. Try to include moments of thought-tracking, allowing the audience to access the inner thoughts and motivations of the characters involved.

STRATEGIES

If you had to change the whole of *Seeds of Survival* into dialogue what characters would you need? Extract the main actions from the text and think about what each character would say. Remember to add stage directions to show the actions and attitudes of the characters. Once you have generated a script you can begin to act. Using your script choose the most significant lines and match them with an action. Mark the most significant action. Look at the pace of the script that you have written and, in rehearsal, try to put pauses in where you think the emotion and tension is high. Play the scene that you have prepared and watch, evaluate and analyse your performance. Use thought-tracking and still images. Comment on the significance of the action and the effectiveness of the elements of drama.

COMMUNICATION

To demand the audience's attention you must understand what you are saying and doing at all times when you are acting. Choose carefully where you are standing and remember every move you make is a sign to the audience. Your audience want to look at a story unfolding; think about using your drama strategies to communicate your key ideas, and play with the structure, plot and arrangement to see what the impact is on the audience. Each person in your group will need a part that shows off their acting skills by sharing the parts. Remember to use your voice to communicate the emotion of the character. Your eye contact with the audience is really important – choose key moments to hold the eye contact and make them listen.

Think tank

When working with a script you will notice that a lot of information has already been given to you. Shakespeare is a master at this. All of his scripts have clear indications of where the characters should be standing and how they should be communicating their lines. Look at the stage directions, the length of the lines, the placing of pauses and the way characters talk to each other. Remember to read a script carefully; firstly, read the script for the narrative (who's who and what's happening). Secondly, look for practicalities (the props and spacing of each character). Thirdly, look at what is being said and how it is being said.

Working with a script can feel restraining at times and you may find it challenging to work practically with a script in your hand. You can nominate one of your peers to read the lines aloud while you work practically in the space; feeding the lines can help prevent a stop/start feeling to your exploration.

Developing your thinking

When you choose a section of script you will need to ask the bigger questions. When working with the *Seeds of Survival* script, ask yourselves the following questions:

- Why is this scene titled as it is?
- What does this title mean?
- What does this child ling to?
- Why will this child survive?

DEVELOPING DRAMA FROM A DEVISED STRUCTURE

ENTRANCES

 Thinking questions

1. Where will you enter from?
2. Who is the character?
3. Where has the character just been?
4. What has just happened to the character?
5. Why is the character entering the space?
6. What time of day is it?
7. What is the space they are entering?
8. Is this a familiar space?
9. What is their response to this space?

MAIN EVENT

 Thinking questions

1. What is the main action that happens in the scene?
2. Who is acting this action?
3. Why are they playing this action?
4. Who is affected by this action?
5. What are their reactions to this action?
6. Has this action happened before?
7. What is the consequence to this action taking place?
8. Will this action happen again?

EXITS

 Thinking questions

1. Where will you exit from?
2. Where are you going to?
3. Why is the character leaving?
4. What will the other characters' reactions be when your character leaves?
5. What will the space be like once you have left?
6. What will the characters true thoughts be once you have left?
7. What action will you do before you leave?
8. What are your thoughts as you leave?
9. Are you being forced to leave?

On the previous page are some thought-provoking questions that will help you create drama that has meaning and depth. You may wish to try mapping out the character's journey on your own. Start at the beginning and walk through the stages that they are going through.

Developing your thinking

When you are devising it is often the process of generating ideas that is very difficult. Try researching Mike Leigh's work, a practitioner who specialises in working with actors through improvisation. He sets up clear character history but does not tell the actors the main events. Some actors may be told some information different to other actors; this sets up a live and spontaneous situation where all the actors are playing their characters but will need to respond to scenarios on the spot.

THEMES

The *Dark Heart* extract on page 33 mentions that the primary school grounds are visited by hooligans at night. Consider the event of breaking into a primary school at night. What are the main themes that can be connected to this event?

◼ Violence   ◼ Crime   ◼ Isolation   ◼ Gangs
◼ Peer pressure   ◼ Pain   ◼ Bullying   ◼ Power.

To create these themes on stage, how could you prepare the space? When you want to prepare a scene, one way is to break the action up into three titles: the entrance; the main event; and the exit. Try creating three still images so that you are clear on what you want to show.

Moving into a still image with a short piece of action before is sometimes referred to as an **action depiction**. Try creating three action depictions showing nighttime tableaux in the school grounds.

STRATEGIES

In order to make it nighttime at the school grounds, or whichever scene you think connects the themes that you are exploring in class, try to include significant actions. Try finishing these sentences to communicate a social message: 'This is a place where …'; 'This is a time when …'; 'I feel …'.

DEVELOPING YOUR THINKING

Look at what is left on the grounds in the morning – see the *Dark Heart: Hidden Britain* extract on page 33 to help you.

◼ What effect do these objects have on the students the next morning?
◼ Why are the young people disaffected with education?
◼ Why are they abusive to their peers, their environment and themselves?

You can approach your work in class not only as a performer but also as:

- **A director** – A director is someone who will rehearse with a group of actors and be able to pick out the most successful moments and help the actors recreate them again. They help and guide the actors in shaping the drama. They will often prepare them by leading exercises that help prepare the actor's voice, body and mind for performance.
- **A designer** – A designer is someone who creates the world of the play. They can work in one discipline: costume, lighting, or set. They may work on the whole design of the drama. They will use drawings, scaled models and mood boards to communicate to the actors their vision of the world of the drama. They can make decisions about what they think would enhance the drama. They, like the director, consult with the actors to make sure that they are all sharing a similar vision.
- **A deviser** – A deviser is someone that focuses on creating the drama. They will work closely with the actors, helping to stimulate ideas and creative ways of constructing a scene. They will use games, props, and imaginative exercises to stimulate the actors' imaginations. They will use storyboards, scripts extracts, poems, pictures, and objects as stimuli to open up all possible opportunities for the actors.

When you work as a team of director, deviser, designer and performer, there will come a time in the rehearsal process where the director will move into a more holistic role and pull the whole performance together. This is not to say that the other roles are redundant, but they will be less significant towards the end of the process as they have helped create, shape and design the drama.

COMMUNICATION

Your audience will need to see three clear scenes that show the story developing alongside the characters. The best way in which to ensure this process is to take photographs on sequence (or film the sequence) to check back that you are communicating what you have planned. Remember you will need to think about how to move from one scene to the next using a transition.

You can communicate through the following drama strategies.

- Action narration
- Soundscape
- Thought-tracking
- Music
- Lighting
- Slow motion
- Choral movement (all moving together)
- Sound Collage.

A **transition** is the word used to describe moving smoothly and creatively from one scene to the next. The most common way to achieve this is through a black out. However, if you think about exploring ways of transitioning in the light, where your audience and examiner can see you, you are opening up more opportunities to gain marks.

? Thinking questions

Think about how you can use lighting to show the school grounds at night. How will the scene look at the beginning compared to the end?

Try thinking about the scene from differing points of view:

- Point of view of the young people involved
- Point of view of the children's parents
- Point of view of primary-school children
- Point of view of a local politician.

How can you include these different points of view in your drama to engage your audience.

Bertolt Brecht created performances that forced the audience to think about the world in which they lived. He hoped that his work would begin to create social change.

How can you create drama that makes your audience think and enacts social change? Ask yourself the following questions:

- Who – if anyone – is to blame for the way these children are?
- Is blame the right response to have?
- How can we attempt to help these children?
- Is helping them the right course of action?
- If there was a punishment or consequence what would that be?
- How would that punishment or consequence prevent this cycle of events?

DEVELOPING DRAMA FROM A POEM

'Timothy Winters' by Charles Causley from *Selected Poems for Children* (Macmillan 1997).

WORKING FROM A POEM

In the left-hand column below, is an example of a poem and on the right-hand side is what a GCSE drama candidate has written in response to reading the poem. You too could choose a poem that relates to the themes that you are exploring in class and make your own comparisons.

Timothy Winters comes to school
With eyes as wide as a football pool,
Ears like bombs and teeth like splinters:
A blitz of a boy is Timothy Winters.
His belly is white, his neck is dark,
And his hair is an exclamation mark.
His clothes are enough to scare a crow
And through his britches the blue winds blow.
When teacher talks he won't hear a word
And he shoots down dead the arithmetic-bird,
He licks the patterns off his plate
And he's not even heard of the Welfare State.
Timothy Winters has bloody feet
And he lives in a house on Suez Street,
He sleeps in a sack on the kitchen floor
And they say there aren't boys like him anymore.
Old Man Winters likes his beer
And his missus ran off with a bombardier,
Grandma sits in the grate with a gin
And Timothy's dosed with an aspirin
The Welfare Worker lies awake
But the law's as tricky as a ten-foot snake,

Timothy Winters seems like a boy that doesn't really have any hopes or dreams and has been alone for most of his life. 'Eyes as wide as a football pool,' suggests that Timothy is tired and could have black rings around his eyes. He is tired because he doesn't sleep perhaps from being uncomfortable.

'Ears like bombs and teeth like splinters.' This line suggests that maybe all that Timothy Winters can hear is war. 'Teeth like splinters,' suggests that he is very thin and unhealthy from not eating. Perhaps what he does eat, his food is so hard and dry that it cuts his teeth into splinters.

In the second stanza, a line that is important is 'his belly is white and his hair is dark,' because it talks of his lack of food again and that his hair is dirty. Starvation is what would turn a belly white.

He doesn't listen to the teachers: 'he shoots down dead the arithmetic-bird.' He has no shoes: 'Timothy Winters has bloody feet,' and he 'sleeps in a sack on the kitchen floor.' This suggests again that he is poor and his family don't provide for him. He cannot make sense of what he is learning in school.

Timothy has an alcoholic guardian, 'Old man winters likes his

So Timothy Winter's drinks his cup
And slowly goes on growing up.
At Morning Prayers the Master helves
For children less fortunate than ourselves,
And the loudest response in the room is when
Timothy Winters roars 'Amen!'
So come one angel, come on ten:
Timothy Winters says 'Amen
Amen amen amen amen.'
Timothy Winters, Lord.

Amen.

beer,' and also the fact that he is 'dosed with an aspirin.' It's almost like his guardians can't be bothered to take care of him; they dose him up so that he sleeps and needs no care or attention.

'The Welfare Worker lies awake.' The welfare workers cannot do anything to help him. They haven't found him as there are so many cases like him but they just pretend it doesn't happen.

'The law's as tricky as a ten-foot snake.' This metaphor suggests that the law is so big and difficult to understand that it's almost impossible to know what is right and wrong. The repetition of 'Amen' in the last two stanzas represents Timothy's hope. He still hopes that he will be saved. It emphasises his faith and belief. He is grateful to still be alive.

THEMES

As you read the poem, circle the words that link directly to the work that you have already been exploring. You have now identified words that connect to the main themes. As you read, try to picture the images that the poem creates in your own mind. These images can be created by you and your classmates and you can take a photo for your documentary response.

STRATEGIES

Using the depictions that you created from the poem, you can now use thought-tracking to communicate to an audience the deeper ideas at work in the poem. This will demand you to think about what these characters are feeling, seeing, hearing and thinking.

Choose a main character that you have come across in the script extract, poem, lyrics or the night in the school grounds devised work, and prepare a piece of drama that demonstrates the children's biggest hope and their worst fear. You can use action depictions to start the process and then layer up the performance with voice, sound, light, costume, and make-up. Try to work non-naturalistically; use movement, symbolism and voicescapes. Draw on work and research that you have completed and reference them in your drama.

COMMUNICATION

From the point of view of:

A **director** – You can begin by setting the scene. As the director you will need to create the world of the play through placing your actors carefully in your chosen acting space. Think carefully about the signs that you are setting up for your audience to read. Your actors will need to think about the motivations of their actions and why they are in the location that you have put them, but you will need to coach them into being in a position that shows the audience their relationship with each other. Think carefully about status, levels and action.

A **designer** – Create the shape and overall look of the piece. Each area of the stage needs to be designed, including props, costumes, set, lighting, and overall image of the production. Working together with the director you are trying to create an overall image. Remember to design a set that works with the actors rather than against them. Try to design a set that is functional and symbolic meaning of the of the play.

A performer – Communicate to the audience through your characterisation. Remember that you are being watched and read by your audience all of the time. Each action, movement and sound you make will be interpreted. Your attention will need to be on your control of voice, movement and action.

A deviser – Develop the text and action. Imagine that you are creating the main character from the poem above; you will need to imagine what their world is like and how they see their environment. As a deviser you could ask your actors to write on to an A5 piece of paper a diary entry of a day in the life of this character. This will generate a lot of text quickly and you will be able to choose the most powerful lines from each of them. Once you have put all of the best lines together, this monologue can be performed by one or more of your actors.

> ### Think tank
>
> Reflecting back over the skills that you are developing, you should now be confident in working with a short extract of text and developing it to a full-length performance. You know to go through the script and choose significant actions, where you can insert drama elements to communicate the deeper meanings. You can now create an episodic scene, work in different roles, use stimulus material, and link your drama to wider social questions.

 ## Thinking questions for Dark Heart

- What can be done to help these children?
- Has society failed these children?
- What will these children carry with them into adulthood?
- Can we effect change in areas and communities such as these?
- Is education today child centred?
- How are the rights of the child demonstrated (or not) in our society today?

Asking these bigger questions will enhance your own understanding of the characters' relationships to the world. The audience will benefit from making connections to what they are seeing on stage to the world outside.

DOCUMENTARY RESPONSE

Remember that your work will need to be identified clearly. Every page of your documentary response must have the following information on it:

- Your name
- *Dark Heart*: Unit 1 Documentary Response [*Write your title with the topic that you have studied*].

■ You must make sure that you justify everything you say
■ You must use the **drama explorative strategies** to describe what you created in class and always say what **drama mediums** you used and what impact they had on your audience.
■ Make sure that you link everything you write to the stimuli you have been working on in class.

GUIDANCE TO HELP YOU WRITE YOUR DOCUMENTARY RESPONSE

The words in red are sentence-starter ideas that you could use to help guide you when you are writing your response. This candidate studied *Dark Heart* for their Unit 1 work.

The guidance that follows is supported by the work of a GCSE candidate who has recorded their responses to the class work that they experienced.

> We were presented with a stimuli pack at the start of this unit of work. I have taken some extracts/pictures from these and will describe what I think they mean and discuss them in detail.

Extract from *Dark Heart* (Chatto and Windus 1997) by Nick Davie

There is a small boy in the playground, probably about eight years old, and he is crying while his young mother stands and looks away. In a flat voice, she says, 'Shut your mouth.' He cries on. 'Shut your mouth!' He cries on. She turns and leans into his face. 'Shut your mouth or I'll slap you.' He shuts his mouth and starts crying through his nose instead, and his mother looks away again.

> This opening to the chapter was quite disturbing. It shocked me as it forced me to think about how children are still treated this way in our society. This opening sums up this child's life and the fact that the parents do not try to comfort them but would rather use harshness and violence as punishment. The fact that these parents don't care and are not able to show love is of great sadness to me.

Developing your thinking

You can take time to research factual information that supports any statements that you make in your written work. An example for the above candidate would be that they could bring in research about a community that is similar to the one in the story and draw comparisons.

Your teacher will have given you the chance to look at a variety of stimuli that are based around a particular theme. The stimuli could range from pictures and poems to lyrics and photographs.

I feel all the pieces of text and starting points were linked to each other in the following ways … *(Discuss the themes that come out of your exploration and the links between them.)*

I feel the pieces of text, pictures and poems in the pack can be linked together in the following ways; they all look at children and how they are mistreated, undervalued and forgotten. The 'Timothy Winters' poem is connected with the *Dark Heart* extract because they both examine children and the poverty that constricts them and the weighted feeling that they can never aspire to anything. This links with *Seeds of Survival*. The child in this hasn't received help from society so they do not bother with society. All three of these also look at how parents treat their children. In 'Timothy Winters', the child hasn't got a family, only two drunk relatives. In *Seeds of Survival*, we don't know what has happened to the child. My guess is that they were thrown out of their house and are now alone or that they have chosen to leave because of so many problems in their house.

The theme of trying to escape from society or home life is a big connection between all this stimulus material. Moreover, the pictures showing anti-social behaviour demonstrate that some people have nowhere else to turn; the only place to find comfort and strength is in a violent gang that have become obsessed with destroying society. The child swearing shows how corrupt children have become learning from their parents about the extremities of verbal and physical abuse. Also, this picture shows how the children of today view the world. They have no respect for society because society doesn't respect them.

As you can see, the candidate has gone through each of the stimuli and connected them with their understanding of the main themes. Make sure that you too highlight the main themes and write how they connect to the stimuli that you have been exploring.

DEVELOPING YOUR UNDERSTANDING OF ROLE AND CHARACTER

Character and role are areas that you will be assessed on practically in class by your teacher, as you will be later in Unit 3, if you choose performing as your main option rather than performance support. Consider how you will communicate your exploration of role in your written response. A role on the wall is a useful way of creating an outline of a person. Inside the outline of a human figure, write the feelings of the character. On the outside, write facts about that character. This is one way of understanding the character that you are studying or playing.

STUDENT RESPONSE

The character study has taught me a lot about the child, for example …

The candidate has clearly shown an understanding of the character. They have described the character's situation, developed their response on that character and then made some links to the world in which we live. This process is a really good model to use for your character/role exploration.

The character study has taught me a lot about this child. For example, I have learnt more about the background of some of these children. This child is being abused by his father. The child can only escape from him at school. I now understand it wasn't the child who set the fire to the house but him making his child do it. This doesn't account for all children but pressure from an adult or parent can cause psychological harm to a child. Guns aren't dangerous until you put someone behind them. It's the same with some children. They're only as dangerous or as violent as society makes them.

Choose the character that you want to describe carefully so that wherever possible you can support your thoughts and opinions with the text or facts that you have researched.

The character study has taught me alot about this child, who had to pretend to be dead in order to survive. This is an example of how cruel society is to these kids. No one should have to pretend to be dead in order to stay alive, especially a child. I think that this child was in a war and was made to fight. They laid down on the floor and stayed completely still as soldiers checked if the dead were really dead. Another theory for this child was that maybe they were living on the streets and saw a gang coming towards them and they laid down there and pretended to be dead. Some of these children have glimpsed at a world with no morals or decency and witnessed things they never should have. Some children have seen more terrifying things in their first few years than some do in their entire lifetime.

EXPLORING AND DEVELOPING MEANING FROM LYRICS

We listened to REM's song *Everybody Hurts*. Here are my responses to the song/music/lyrics …

We listened to REM's song *Everybody Hurts*. Here is my response to the song, the music and the lyrics. I thought that the lyrics offer a pertinent comparison to the *Dark Heart: Hidden Britain* book. In our work in role, we used this song as the lyrics relate to the book's children. I have highlighted the key lines:

REM: *Everybody Hurts*
When the day is long and the night, the night is yours alone,
When you're sure you've had enough of this life, well hang on.
Don't let yourself go, everybody cries and everybody hurts sometimes
Sometimes everything is wrong. Now it's time to sing along
When your day is night, if you feel like letting go,
When you think you've had too much of this life, well hang on.
Everybody hurts. Take comfort in your friends.
Everybody hurts. Don't throw your hand. Oh no. Don't throw your hand.
If you feel like you're alone, no, no, no, you're not alone.
If you think you're on your own in this life, these days and nights are long,
When you think you've had too much of this life to hang on.
Well everybody hurts sometimes.
Everybody cries. And everybody hurts sometimes.

And everybody hurts sometimes. So, hold on, hold on.
Hold on, hold on, hold on, hold on, hold on.
Everybody hurts. **You are not alone**.

The children in *Dark Heart: Hidden Britain* feel like they have had too much of their lives. This song is about hanging on. Everybody does hurt sometime in their life whether it is from a family death, a physical affliction or an emotional problem. All of these things happen to us and there are people that you can turn to, like your friends. They are there to comfort you. The line 'Sometimes everything is wrong' is about the world in general and how society can be wrong. Parents hit their children; raping, murder and gang violence all take place routinely. 'Now it's time to sing along,' means that now we all need to set our differences aside and get along. 'These days and nights are long,' has a strong connection to these children because everyday they are put through mental tests that are hard. It causes them pain. 'You are not alone,' is a line which sums up the whole song. No one is alone and there is always someone that can help you. This song is all about the realisation that hope does exist in others.

Developing your thinking

You may have been given a set of song lyrics from your teacher, but if not you can introduce your own. You will be showing initiative and the ability to connect different stimuli independently from your teacher. The candidate has highlighted the lyrics that they felt meant the most in relation to the other stimuli that they have been exploring. This is a good technique to use for your documentary response.

DEVELOPING THE WORK YOU HAVE EXPLORED IN CLASS

Here is a diary entry from one of the children living on the sink estate the night after their first assembly:

The children were asked to produce a piece of writing titled 'My school'. Here is what one candidate wrote:

My school is the best. I get up every morning bright and early with a smile on my face. Mondays are the best for everyone but especially me. When I get here on a Monday I know that I have survived another weekend at home. No more suffering at least for another six hours. School is heaven in my mind. My parents don't encourage school and never took any interest but I loved it from the first day I got here.

I get taken here everyday by my mum. We always stop at this alleyway where my mother talks to this stranger. Whenever I ask her what she's doing she says, 'Shut up and wait. I just need a quick fix.' I never really knew what she meant. Then as we got closer I started smiling, especially where I could see the big gates with a bra hanging off and a used balloon put over a spike. I remember I used to run across the wall half way down the road until one day my mother told me I couldn't anymore. 'Why mum?', 'Because I said so?' Then she slapped me. That was when she started getting fixes I think.

Now I don't care what she does because I know that when I get in those gates, when I cross that line, she can't touch me. A glistening coat of protection will cover me. However, it can only keep me safe for so long. At those bars at 3 o'clock, my mother will wait. The last minute before we leave at the end of the day, those smiles disappear and drip off of our faces. In the last minute we suck up what is left of happiness. Then we leave until tomorrow. Walking home to hell. What keeps me going is this school. Please don't take it away.

You need to annotate your writing in role to say why you have written what you have and what you have learnt from it. Below a candidate has explained each decision that they made. They have been really careful to point out the language and words they chose to express the character's view of the world.

I chose to write this because I thought that this child was totally dependent on their school to escape the troubles of their home life. Their case is exactly like all the other children. They all love their school because it is where they are most comforted and have sanctuary. They get away from their parents. I also chose to refer to the gate having a 'bra' and a 'balloon' on it, which refers back to the teenagers going there at night and trashing the building. They know their school gets trashed but they don't understand why or what these 'balloons' are. My character here tells that her mother gets fixes, referring to heroin. I put this child in my documentary response to show how these children observe what happens around them but just don't understand it.

Developing your thinking

Choose a character from the work that you have been exploring. You could even choose a character that is not necessarily a central character – a person of authority, such as a school nurse, community doctor, bus driver, or post-person. Whichever you choose, think of the language, register and style so that you are taking every advantage to express to your reader what this character is like.

After working on the themes and exploring the context of the stimuli pack, I would look at the texts and photographs differently. This is what I have learnt from the practical exploration that I would apply to them …

Developing your thinking

The candidate has covered all of required the areas in detail. They have taken the opportunity to reflect and evaluate their thinking and perceptions and how they have changed over the course of the unit. Make sure that you too look over the notes that you have made before you embark on putting the whole documentary response together. It is vital you reflect, analyse and evaluate.

I think while I look at the pictures that I understand more about the children. The children are all sad and disturbed because of a government that has left them for dead. They no longer respect society because that society no longer respects its children.

The texts in the pack give an overview of the unit. They sum up our society, which leaves so many children out. Parents and adults have become so independent that they no longer have time for their children.

In a developing world, the only way you can survive is if you earn as much money as possible. It is so hard for the children today to find high-paid areas of employment unless they can spend money in higher education. How will these children get good jobs when they have no money to begin with? They can't pay to got to college or university and the government won't pay the fees for them.

Through practical exploration I have learnt about these children. When I see a child like this I will think about what they have had to go through and what their life must be like.

Think tank

During this unit you will have explored topics, themes and issues. You will have worked with stimuli ranging from poetry to newspaper or magazine articles. You will have gained new skills and enhanced existing skills in how to develop a meaningful piece of drama that has an impact on an audience. You are now ready to progress to Unit 2.

PRACTICAL EXPLORATION OF A COMPLETE PLAY TEXT: EQUUS

CAROL ROSEGG

You will read and study a play that has been chosen by your teacher. You will explore the way the play has been written and question the impact it would have on an audience. You will analyse the playwright's intentions and discover the deeper meanings beneath the text, characters and context. You will respond, reflect and evaluate on the themes and issues that the play deals with as well as developing your performance skills. You will see a live performance of a play, either in your school or at the theatre, that you will write a 2,000 word critical review of.

Unit 2 focuses on the way you read and interpret a play and how you can use your drama explorative strategies and drama mediums to communicate meaning to an audience.

Extract from *Equus* (Penguin 1977), Act 1 scene 1, page 42

Dysart: With one particular horse, called Nugget, he embraces. The animal digs its sweaty brow into his cheek, and they stand in the dark for an hour – like a necking couple. And of all nonsensical things – I keep thinking about the *horse*! Not the boy: the horse, and what it may be trying to do. I keep seeing that huge head kissing him with its chained mouth. Nudging through the metal some desire absolutely irrelevant to fillings its belly or propagating its own kind. What desire could that be? Not to stay a horse any longer? Not to remain reined up for ever in those particular genetic strings? Is it possible, at certain moments we cannot imagine, a horse can add its sufferings together – the non-stop jerks and jabs that are its daily life – and turn them into grief? What use is grief to a horse?

💬 A **script** is the printed dialogue and stage directions on which a performance is based. The stage directions are as much part of the play as the dialogue. You need to decide whether you will follow the stage directions written by the playwright or whether you will work to communicate the meaning you think they contain in a different way.

There are many phrases in the text extract above that convey Dysart's confusion, doubt and sense of helplessness. Look at all the questions Dysart asks, and think about what the playwright is telling the audience about the character of Dysart through his use of language.

Think tank

For Unit 2, your teacher will give you a whole play text to explore through drama. It is important that you read the whole text, even though you will only work on sections of it. The internet is also a useful source of information about the play. Use search engines to find details about the original production and also productions that may be happening at the moment. Visual images, set designs, and posters from past productions are all useful ways into the text.

Developing your thinking

In any search engine, type in the subject you are looking for; in this case *Equus*, the play. Have a look at the first five or six documents that are presented to you. Using the internet for research can be very valuable, but this does not mean just printing off piles of paper and bringing those in to your drama lesson. It means firstly reading through the information on screen to see if it is useful. It then means selecting specific sections of the information and using just this selection. Read through the information again, making your own notes on a separate piece of paper or around the edges of the printed text. You might also highlight some interesting sections of the printed text, or sections that you don't understand and will ask your teacher to help you with.

Developing your thinking

As you read a play text, it is important that you make detailed notes. One way of doing this would be to record your thoughts after each scene, recording your reflections under the following headings: plot, subplot, themes, symbolism, development of character, and staging ideas.

THEMES

At the centre of the play is the true incident of a 17-year-old boy called Alan Strang, who committed the terrible act of blinding six horses with a metal spike. Alan's act of violence is an extreme act, and he is treated in hospital by Dr Martin Dysart, a man who feels his life has become mundane and ordinary. He feels his existence is passionless, whereas he views Alan as a young man full of passion, albeit misplaced. Note down what you regard as the major themes of *Equus* and then share these with others. In small groups, you may want to prepare still images for three or four of these major themes – these can be naturalistic or abstract or a mixture of the two. When you share these with the class, think about your transitions between the still images.

? Thinking questions

- Why do you think Alan acted the way he did?
- Can society in any way be held accountable for Alan's actions?
- How does Alan's crime make you feel?

DRAMA STRATEGIES

Read the playwright's notes on the setting. Draw the set as described by Peter Shaffer on page 1 of the play text *Equus*:

> A square of wood set on a circle of wood... the square is set on ball bearings... on the square are set two little plain benches... in the area outside the circle stand benches. Two downstage left and right are curved to accord with the circle... benches accommodate the actors (who sit on stage)... the entire evening. Upstage, forming a backdrop to the whole, are tiers of seats in the fashion of a dissecting theatre, formed into two railed-off blocks, pierced by a central tunnel. To left and right, downstage, stand two ladders on which are suspended horse masks.

It is always a useful starting point to reflect upon how the author describes the setting. In your interpretation of the text, you may choose to change some of the visual elements that are listed in the drama mediums in your syllabus. Revise examples of the drama mediums on page 14.

Marking the moment is a convention used to sign to the audience a significant moment in the drama. You could use drama strategies like freeze-framing or narration or you might employ drama mediums like spotlighting, sound effects, musical underscoring or a change in lighting.

Around the edges of the set, add notes about the meaning and the symbolism contained in each element. We are now analysing the **mise-en-scène**. The word mise-en- scène is a French term and literally means 'what is put in the scene'. It can be seen as the arrangement of scenery, props, and actors on the stage.

 Thinking questions

■ Why is the colour of the set important? What does it symbolise?
■ Why is it important that the audience watch from the front and not from behind?
■ Why does Shaffer suggest a raised central area? What does this provide the audience with?
■ Why does Shaffer say the lights will be visible to the audience? What effect will this have on them?

As a way of dissecting any piece of text you might read a sentence out loud and then another actor could say:

■ Why the character says that line
■ What the character feels when they say that line
■ How the character says the line.

Read the opening monologue by Dysart on page 58 and dissect the text in this way.

Think tank

A strategy to explore character is hot-seating. This is when you are in role and, without any preparation, you answer questions about yourself. It is important that you become the character rather than just telling the audience about the character. Focus on their physicality and how they hold themselves; maybe they have a twitch or a repeatable physical habit. Just because your teacher doesn't mention hot-seating when you are asked to develop a character, you may choose to employ this strategy yourself if you think it will deepen your understanding of the character.

What do you think is the most important section of this opening text? You are going to mark this moment. Think about how you will make that moment significant to your audience and how you will highlight its importance. Discuss the visual, aural and spatial elements and then stage that moment employing drama mediums.

Ensure you note down all the drama strategies that you have used and employed.

■ Name and then describe the strategy
■ Say why you used it
■ Say what you learnt from using it.

COMMUNICATION

You are now outside the court where Alan is being tried for his crime looking at the boy. Use the rubric below to respond to Alan as either a character from the play or a member of the public; you may choose to finish one or all of the sentences:

- ◼ I see in front of me ... (*abstract or naturalistic*)
- ◼ I hear around me ...
- ◼ In my heart I feel ...
- ◼ I know ...

Then extend your scene. Have Dysart step forward and complete the above rubric. Use the rest of your group to prepare still images behind him revealing how he feels about each sentence response.

Remember to make a note of your scene in your notebook. Also make a note of your evaluation of other people's performance. Be sure to comment on:

- ◼ What you have learnt about Dysart through watching the scenes
- ◼ What you have learnt about how society responds to crime and violence.

Developing your thinking

Do an internet search using Peter Shaffer as your key words. Find a biography of Peter Shaffer so you understand what Shaffer has done in the past, what sort of life he has led and what other plays he has written.

Think tank

You are now beginning to understand how a play text needs to be interpreted in different ways in order for it to be performed. You have begun the process of understanding what actors, designers and directors have to do and the decisions they have to make to turn a play text into performance.

Extract from *Equus* (Penguin 1977), Act 1 scene 3, page 44

Alan (singing low): Double your pleasure

Double your fun

With Doublemint, Doublemint

Doublemint gum.

Dysart (unperturbed): Now, let's see. You work in an electrical shop during the week. You live with your parents, and your father's a printer. What sort of things does he print?

Alan (singing louder): Double your pleasure

Double your fun

With Doublemint, Doublemint

Doublemint gum.

Dysart: I mean does he do leaflets and calendars. Things like that?

The boy approaches him, hostile.

Alan (singing): Try the taste of Martini

The most beautiful drink in the world.

It's the right one –

The bright one –

That's Martini!

Dysart: I wish you'd sit down, if you're going to sing. Don't you think you'd be more comfortable?

Pause.

Alan (singing): There's only one T in Typhoo!

In packets and teabags too.

Any way you make it, you'll find it's true:

There's only one T in Typhoo!

Dysart (appreciatively): Now that's a good song. I like it better than the other two. Can I hear that one again?

Alan starts away from him, and sits on the upstage bench.

Alan (singing): Double your pleasure

Double your fun

With Doublemint, Doublemint

Doublemint gum.

Dysart (smiling): You know I was wrong. I really do think that one's better. It's got such a catchy tune. Please do that one again.

The text spoken by Alan is taken from advert jingles from television commercials that were popular at the time the playwright wrote this text – commercials for chewing gum, the drink Martini, tea and petrol. Would you want to change what jingles Alan sings to update the text or would you want to keep the context of the text in the early 1970s?

Think tank

What are your initial impressions of Alan and Dysart? How does the audience's attitude towards Alan develop during this scene? To what extent can we sympathise with him in spite of our knowledge of what he has done? What are the various ways in which we learn about Alan during these scenes? Does Alan appear to be mentally unbalanced? If so, in what ways?

This page focuses on developing our understanding of the character of Martin Dysart using the explorative strategies of: narrating, thought-tracking, role-play, forum-theatre, marking the moment and movement.

THEMES

Who do you think is the central character in this play text? It would be easy to say Alan Strang, but if you look at the text carefully, the play is also exploring the character of Martin Dysart and how he compares his life to the life of Alan. Dysart is representative of a society that is trying to make Alan 'normal' again.

 Thinking questions

- What is normal?
- Why would Dysart be jealous of Alan Strang?
- Compare the two characters. What has Dysart got that Alan hasn't, and what has Alan got that Dysart wants?
- What has Dysart's life become?

BUILDING A DRAMATIC SPACE FOR THE CHARACTER

Mark out the space with tape or with rope laid out in a square on the floor. This is Dysart's office or consulting room. We are building this naturalistically; how is this different to the author's intention?

Lay out all the objects in the office. Objects might include:

- Desk (what's on it?)
- Chair
- Sofa
- Comfy chair
- Window
- Door
- Picture on wall (what of?)
- Greek mask on wall

Add in any other objects you think are important.

Developing your thinking

It would be a good idea to draw the set. You might do this as a ground plan, a view from above showing where all the objects are, or you might draw the set in 3D. If your teacher will let you, you might use your mobile phone to take a picture of the set to use in your notebook. Your teacher might take a photo with a digital camera. Once you have recorded the setting, make sure you annotate your decision; write next to each object what its significance is and why it is there.

Think about what the most significant object in the space is, and how you can ensure that proxemically this object is significant within the mise-en-scene. What is its significance to Dysart?

DRAMA STRATEGIES

Narrating is an excellent explorative technique. A narrator is a role that functions like a story-teller for the audience. A narrator can be useful when they describe the action, which allows us to focus in and reflect in detail on what the characters are doing; an action narration is a narration that focuses in on the action. As a whole class you could begin to prepare an action narration. Dysart has heard that Alan is to be sent to him, and he is awaiting his arrival in his office. Action narrate what he does. You could mark significant moments by freezing the action and thought tracking the character. You could also develop the layers of meaning for some of his more significant actions. Layers of meaning are an excellent explorative technique that allow us to focus in on the most important actions in a sequence.

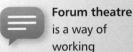

Forum theatre is a way of working developed by Brazilian theatre practitioner, Augusto Boal. His work centres around the idea of involvement; if you involve someone in an activity then they are more likely to understand what you are showing them.

There are five layers of meaning in an action developed by drama practitioner, Dorothy Heathcote:

■ ACTION – what are you doing?
■ MOTIVATION – why are you doing that?
■ INVESTMENT – what do you get from doing that?
■ MODEL – where have you seen or used this action before?
■ STANCE – what is the world like to you in this moment?

You may employ forum theatre during the action narration. If, as you work through, you are unhappy with a suggestion or action, you can stop the action and re-direct or suggest alternatives. Through these explorative strategies you will be building up your understanding of the character of Martin Dysart and what is important to him. As a way of recording the character choices you are making, construct a role on the wall for Martin Dysart. Inside the image write everything he is sure of; outside of the image write everything he is unsure of.

Gesture is part of the semiotics of theatre. A gesture is a movement of a part of the body, especially a hand or the head, that conveys meaning or an idea to an audience.

Ensure you note down all the drama strategies that you have used and employed:

■ Name and describe the strategy
■ Say why you used it
■ Say what you learnt from using it

COMMUNICATION

On- and off- text exercises. While you are exploring a play text practically your teacher will ask you to take part in on-text exercises. These are exercises you will undertake using the text directly. Examples might include: still images, thought-tracking, hot-seating, breaking the text into units of action, developing emotional memory connections between actor and character, or maybe exploring the subtext of the scene. Off-text exercises are rehearsal exercises used when the actor is not following the text. Any improvisation you undertake that places characters in different contexts is off-text work.

You are now developing a scene that uses various drama mediums. These could include space and the use of levels, set and props, movement and gestures. You are marking a significant moment in the narrative of the text. What do you regard as a major turning point between Dysart and Alan in the text? This is where your own action narrations happen; Dysart is left alone after this chosen incident.

Prepare an action narration that includes:

- Thought tracks
- Speaking layers of meaning
- Significant action
- Significant objects and their use
- Some lines from the text.

Remember to make a note of your scene in your notebook. Also make a note of your evaluation of other people's performance. Be sure to comment on:

- Whether this action narration gives us further insight into the moment chosen and the character of Martin Dysart
- The use of significant props and objects. Did the use of these props extend communication of meaning to the audience or where they just cluttering the space?

Think tank

What you have now explored is how to use significant props and objects to communicate meaning to an audience. You have also constructed a naturalistic setting for a scene. When you discuss the setting make sure you do not just describe the scene, but that you analyse your decisions. This means telling your examiner the reasons behind your choices, and what effect you were intending and what you hoped to sign to your audience. These are all useful techniques, not just for studying this text, but for any text your teacher may give you.

Why is Dysart so fascinated with this story in the extract from *Equus* above? After each meeting, where Dysart learns more about Alan Strang, he would write up his case notes. This is a useful off-text exercise to do. Writing in role, complete Dysart's case notes after hearing this story from Dora. Writing in role helps you deepen your understanding of the events in the text.

The focus of this page is significance of object – how you build significance and how you communicate this to your audience. The practical work will also use layers of meaning in an action. The strategies and mediums used include: still image, thought-tracking, narrating, use of movement, mime or gesture, and use of spoken language.

Extract from *Equus* (Penguin 1977), Act 1 scene 11, page 46

Dora: It was a reproduction of Our Lord on his way to Calvary. Alan found it in Reeds Art Shop, and fell absolutely in love with it. He insisted on buying it with his pocket money, and hanging it at the foot of his bed where he could see it last thing at night. My husband was very displeased.

Dysart: Because it was religious?

Dora: In all fairness I must admit it was a little extreme. The Christ was loaded down with chains, and the centurions were really laying on the stripes. It certainly would not have been my choice, but I don't believe in interfering too much with children, so I said nothing.

Dysart: But Mr Strang did?

Dora: He stood it for a while, but one day we had one of our tiffs about religion, and he went straight upstairs, tore it off the boy's wall and threw it in the dustbin. Alan went quite hysterical. He cried for days without stopping – and he was not a crier, you know.

Dysart: But he recovered when he was given the photograph of the horse in its place?

Dora: He certainly seemed to. At least, he hung it in exactly the same position, and we had no more of that awful weeping.

Think tank

This is a very powerful episode in the text. Dora tells Dysart of an incident from Alan's past. The film version of this play chose to actually show this incident as a flashback. A flashback is a moment from the character's past that is re-enacted and remembered. A flashback can provide some back story for the character and communicate to the audience the character's behaviour and feelings. Through using a flashback, the audience build up their understanding of character.

THEMES

The text extract above focuses on the major themes of religion and people's search for meaning in their lives. It is always useful to identify the text's major themes as early as possible; you might revise your choices as you go along, which is okay. In your notebooks, write down the major themes of the text, and collect quotations under these different headings as you read the text.

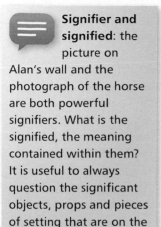

Signifier and signified: the picture on Alan's wall and the photograph of the horse are both powerful signifiers. What is the signified, the meaning contained within them? It is useful to always question the significant objects, props and pieces of setting that are on the stage.

Revise Dorothy Heathcote's layers of meaning in an action on page 64.

In Units 1 and 2 the work you produce is not intended for performance to a theatre audience, although you may choose to take some of the scenes you have produced as a starting point for your work for Unit 3. Have a quick look now at the discussion about a hybrid performance on page 109. It is important to remember that part of the process of sharing your work with your class is to respond to constructive feedback. Also, evaluating other people's drama in class will build up the skills you require to write an evaluation of an experience of live theatre as a member of the audience.

EXPLORING THE MEANING OF ALAN'S PICTURE

You are working in role as either Alan, Frank or Dora. Imagine the picture of 'the Christ, our Lord, loaded down with chains.' Establish what you all imagine the picture to be like. Working in role, finish the sentence:

■ I see in front of me …

 Thinking questions

■ What is Shaffer making us think about organised religion?
■ What is Shaffer making us think about the idea of worship?
■ What is Shaffer making us think about the idea of belief?
■ What are the differences between these three words: religion, worship and belief?
■ Do we need 'belief' in our lives?

DRAMA STRATEGIES

The text tells us that Mr Strang '… went straight upstairs, tore [*the picture*] off the boy's wall and threw it in the dustbin'. We will use drama strategies to mark the moment. These techniques can be used to explore the significant action in any scene you read.

As Mr Strang, you are ripping the picture down. While you repeat this action, complete the five layers of meaning in an action.

■ Action   ■ Motivation   ■ Investment   ■ Model   ■ Stance

Between each layer, Mrs Strang naturalistically tells Mr Strang why his action is a bad idea. After each of Mrs Strang's interventions, Alan tells his father why he doesn't want the picture removed.

 Thinking questions

Reflect on what we have learnt about Mr Strang's character – why did he remove the picture? Reflect on how the tension between the parents affects Alan's view of the picture and religion. A role-on-the-wall will reveal some further information about Mr Strang. Inside write what he is really thinking and feeling about the picture, his son and his wife. Outside the image, write what he wants his wife and son to feel as he rips down the picture.

Ancient Greece provides some very rich history in drama. The word drama comes from the Ancient Greek word meaning 'to do'. Drama and theatre were important parts of Greek life, with comedies and tragedies staged in the outdoor amphitheatres as part of the Festival of Dionysus. We get many theatrical words from Ancient Greece including the word thespian which today means an actor. A man named Thespis is said to have invented the concept of the actor.

Extract from *Equus* (Penguin 1977), Act 1, page 48

Dysart: That night, I had this very explicit dream. In it I'm chief priest in Homeric Greece. I'm wearing a wide gold mask, all noble and bearded, like the so-called Mask of Agamemnon found at Mycenae. I'm standing by a thick round stone and holding a sharp knife. In fact, I'm officiating at some immensely important ritual sacrifice, on which depends the fate of the crops or of a military expedition. The sacrifice is a herd of children: about 500 boys and girls. I can see them stretching away in a long queue, right across the plain of Argos. I know it's Argos because of the red soil. On either side of me stand two assistant priests, wearing masks as well: lumpy, pop-eyed masks, such as also were found at Mycenae. They are enormously strong, these other priests, and absolutely tireless. As each child steps forward, they grab it from behind and throw it over the stone. Then, with a surgical skill which amazes even me, I fit in the knife and slice elegantly down to the navel, just like a seamstress following a pattern. I part the flaps, sever the inner tubes, yank them out and throw them hot and steaming on to the floor.

This monologue is filled with words that paint strong images in the audience's minds. It is an emotive speech in that it rouses emotions in the audience. What emotions does this speech make you feel?

Developing your thinking

Do some internet research. Use Ancient Greek theatre as your key words and see what other information you can find out about how plays were staged in Ancient Greece. Find the names of other Ancient Greek playwrights and the plays they wrote. Find a picture of an ancient Greek amphitheatre.

Think tank

This monologue gives us a deeper understanding of the character of Martin Dysart. He has reached a point in his career where he sees no changes in the future. He is beginning to question what he is doing to the young people he attempts to 'heal' and is questioning what he is actually removing from them. Is it their individuality, their passion, the part of them that makes them unique? Dysart also has a love of ancient Greek history and this is clearly linked to the setting of his vivid dream.

THEMES

The essential question is, what does the dream mean? In the dream Dysart is literally cutting out and removing the insides of children. It is interesting to link this to what Dysart does as a job. As a psychiatrist his job is to attempt to heal and to calm their minds and their thoughts. Metaphorically what do you think he is removing from the children?

The focus of this page is the spoken language employed by Shaffer. He uses language to paint some very vivid images in the audience's mind. Unit 2 asks you to develop your understanding of the ways in which playwrights record their ideas in a script, and this scene is an excellent example of how the spoken word is used to conjure pictures for the audience.

💬 A **metaphor** is a technique of drawing a parallel between one thing and another. It is useful to look for metaphors in play texts and in performance. A metaphor maybe contained within the language of the text or a director may choose metaphorical images on the stage to communicate meaning to the audience.

💡 *Developing your thinking*

Dysart is masked in his dream. He is wearing a wide gold mask. This strikes an impressive image in the mind. Drama is a visual art form and it would be useful to collect together some pictures and images representing what the mask looks like for you.

See discussion of Artaudian techniques on page 20 and 22.

Thinking questions

?
- Why is Dysart masked in his dream?
- What does Dysart hide behind in his real life?
- A mask can either conceal or disguise. What is Dysart trying to conceal in his life? Why would Dysart want to disguise himself in the dream?

DRAMA ELEMENTS

Look at the extract from the Dysart monologue and decide where you would put pauses. When an actor pauses the audience's attention is drawn to what they have just said. Where do you want to focus the audience's attention? Think about the pace of the speech. Where do you want the pace to race along so one sentence follows another in quick succession? This way you will take the audience's attention with you during your monologue. Think about the tone of the speech. Through use of tone you will communicate with your audience – you will let them know what you feel about what you are saying – at what points are you angry, excited, scared or in wonder?

Think about your volume and your projection. Do you want your audience to have to work hard to hear what you are saying, do you want to bring the volume down so what you are saying becomes private and secretive, or do you want to bring up your level of projection because you want to share what you are saying, or you are proud of what you are doing? Work through the monologue and think about vocal qualities. Perform the monologue to the rest of the class.

COMMUNICATION

Think about soundscape; this is where you recreate the sounds and atmosphere of the monologue. Soundscaping involves using the voice to recreate the different sounds that you associate with the atmosphere of the monologue. Think about your actor/audience boundary. Where do you want your audience? How can you include them within the action of the scene? How will you communicate to the audience how Dysart is feeling behind the mask? How will you create the shape and sound of 500 children waiting/knowing/seeing what is about to happen to them – why do they not run? How will you show the people watching – what are they seeing/feeling?

Think tank

You have now taken a monologue and broken down the use of language within the text. You have also explored how you can communicate the meaning created by the text to the audience. You have explored linguistic and non-linguistic metaphor and understood how a director can take meaning from a monologue and transfer that into stage images.

Tragedy is a theatrical genre. It is a serious drama in which the action of the play results in the suffering or the death of the main characters. A tragedian is an actor who plays tragic roles.

Think tank

This is a drama experiment. What you are trying to do is mix two texts together. It is a useful exercise to find other pieces of text, extracts from plays or whole play texts, that are linked to the text you are using for your practical exploration. The extract overleaf is translated from a Greek tragedy called *Oedipus the King* written by a playwright called Sophocles. Martin Dysart says he wants to discover the 'real Greece', so it seems appropriate to reflect upon an extract from a Greek play.

Oedipus the King by Sophocles
(translated by Ian Johnston, Richer Resource Publications)

he ripped the golden brooches
she wore as ornaments, raised them high,
and drove them deep into his eyeballs,
crying as he did so: "You will no longer see
all those atrocious things I suffered,
the dreadful things I did! No. You have seen
those you never should have looked upon,
and those I wished to know you did not see.
So now and for all future time be dark!"
With these words he raised his hand and struck,
not once, but many times, right in the sockets.
With every blow blood spurted from his eyes
down on his beard, and not in single drops,
but showers of dark blood spattered like hail.

Hamartia is a tragic flaw. It is a word that comes from ancient Greece. In *Equus*, which character do you think has a tragic flaw? The character themselves may act nobly but be damned by circumstance. Which character fits this description?

Sophocles was a Greek playwright who lived and worked in Athens. Sophocles first produced *Oedipus* in Athens around 430 BC at the principal theatre festival – The Great Dionysia – which was held in honour of the god Dionysus. Aristotle, a Greek philosopher, said this play was the greatest tragedy ever written. At the end of the play Oedipus, King of Thebes, learns many truths about his past and the events that have bought him to where he is today. On learning these truths, Oedipus blinds himself so he no longer has to look upon the evils of the world and so he can not see the results of his previous actions. The speech above by the Chorus is delivered at the moment Oedipus blinds himself. There is a great deal of material about the play and the story on the web if you want to take the study of this play further.

Think tank

There are so many links between Oedipus and *Equus*, between the techniques employed in Greek tragedy and those employed in *Equus*. There are also links between the layout of an ancient Greek amphitheatre and the design ideas Shaffer presents us with. We will explore all these links on the next page. Oedipus blinds himself against the horrors of the world, so he does not have to witness evil anymore. It is interesting to think about the motivation behind Alan's blinding of the horses; why does he blind his god?

What you are now doing is looking at drama from another culture and time period.

THEMES

This extract is taken from a Greek tragedy. Aristotle was an ancient Greek philosopher who first defined tragedy around 330 B.C. He believed tragedy should include:

Noble characters Tragedies traditionally include characters such as gods, kings and characters that are larger than life.	Can you see any links between this and the play text *Equus*? What noble characters appear in *Equus*?
Magnitude Referring to important, heavy and weighty subject matter.	Do you think the subject matter of *Equus* could be said to have magnitude?
Enhanced language Elements of the text should be written in a heightened form, in a poetic style of language.	Do you think the language is Dysart's dream could be said to be enhanced language? Are there any other sections of the text that can be said to be written in enhanced language?
Catharsis Dramatic tension within the plot which makes the audience feel strong emotions and then calms and settles them by the end of the play with a strong conclusion.	Do you think the audience for *Equus* will feel strong emotions? Plot the emotions the audience will feel for each scene. Have a look at the end of this text; do you think the emotions will be calmed by Dysart's speech?

A **prologue** is a speech, often in poetic language, that is addressed to the audience at the beginning of a play. An epilogue is a speech addressed to the audience at the end of a play.

CAN EQUUS BE DEFINED AS A TRAGEDY?

Below is a list of typical dramatic techniques employed in a tragedy as defined by Aristotle. Can you find these techniques reflected in *Equus*?

■ Emotions such as jealousy, grief, anger, sadness

■ A protagonist who is a tragic hero ■ A fatal flaw ■ A prologue

■ Episodes ■ Monologues ■ Dialogues ■ Difficult choices

■ Consequences ■ Clear ending

DRAMA MEDIUMS

Tragedy has its earliest beginnings in Athens. The main theatre outside of Athens could seat an audience of 15,000.

The theatres in ancient Greece were in the open air to utilise the natural sun light so performances could take place during the day. The orchestra was a circular dancing area at the front of the performance area and was used for the Chorus. Dysart is fascinated by ancient Greek history and it seems that Shaffer is taking ideas from ancient Greek theatre and using them in the design for his set. The semi-circle *theatron*, where the audience would sit, has echoes of Shaffer's design ideas for his own text; he states he wants his audience sat in tiered seating in front of and around the sides and back of the acting area.

A Greek tragedy would feature a Chorus (approximately 12-15 performers) who may narrate the story or comment on the action. Shaffer mentions a 'chorus' in his introduction to the text - all the actors humming, thumping and stamping to produce a choric effect to sign to the audience the presence of Equus the god. The group of horses also form elements of a Chorus.

Masks were frequently used in Greek tragedies and it is interesting to note that Dysart is fascinated by ancient Greek history, and that Shaffer himself has used some of the techniques of an ancient Greek tragedy in the structure of his play *Equus*; the actors playing the horses in *Equus* are masked and act like a Greek Chorus in the play.

COMMUNICATION

Return now to the scene you developed in response to Dysart's dream (see page 68).

Is there any way you can work to include lines, sections, extracts from the text of *Oedipus* presented on page 70?

A definition of **normal** is – conforming to the standard, regular, or usual – free from mental disorder.

Think tank

You are now beginning to present complex drama. You have taken a monologue from your play text and have picked out the key themes and images created by the playwright. You have then found another text that has links to the main play text you are exploring, and you have found extracts from that that you have placed within your own drama.

This is the epilogue of the play, and Shaffer attempts to provide answers for the questions that have been raised throughout the text. What is normal? What is Dysart cutting away from his patients? What emotional journey has Dysart gone on from the start of the play until now? The question for the audience and for you has to be – what will become of Alan now?

Extract from *Equus* (Penguin 1977), Act 1 scene 35, page 52

Dysart: I'll heal the rash on his body. I'll erase the welts cut into his mind by flying manes. When that's done, I'll set him on a nice mini-scooter and send him puttering off into the Normal world where animals are treated properly: made extinct, or put into servitude, or tethered all their lives in dim light, just to feed it! I'll give him the good Normal world where we're tethered beside them – blinking our nights away in a non-stop drench of cathode-ray over our shrivelling heads! I'll take away his Field of Ha Ha, and give him the Normal places for his ecstasy – multi-lane highways driven through the guts of cities, extinguishing Place altogether, *even the idea of Place*! He'll trot on his metal pony tamely through the concrete evening – and one thing I promise you: he will never touch hide again!

This epilogue is delivered as direct address; this is when a character talks directly to an audience. This involves the character treating the audience as if they are part of the play, asking questions of them, including them within the action. A direct address breaks down the actor/audience boundary created by the fourth wall.

Dysart says: 'What is normal? The normal is the good smile in a child's eyes – all right. It is also the dead stare in a million adults – it both sustains and kills.'

Developing your thinking

Try to observe the way the actors are using the significant objects and where they are placed on the stage. Your skills in reading the semiotics and interpreting meaning is vital to achieving a high grade. There is no right or wrong answer; it is your opinion and interpretation supported by the text and your knowledge of the play.

Think tank

This scene finally allows us to hear what Dysart feels about Alan. He is full of regret and tells Hesther – the character that first bought Alan to Dysart and who acts as his sounding board throughout the play – what he is making Alan become. He is making him into a 'normal citizen', and this raises many questions for the audience; what is normal? What is it to be a human being in our society today? What do we have to suppress in order to fit in? Dysart almost makes us feel sorry for Alan when we consider what Dysart is turning him into, but we must remember the horrific crimes Alan has committed.

THEMES

How would you define 'normal'? A thought shower will help focus your ideas here. It is always useful to reflect upon the key themes of a scene, and thought showers are an easy way of getting your ideas down on paper, and responding quickly to give immediate answers. It is important what you do with these ideas afterwards and how you write about them in your documentary response and use them in your drama.

STUDENT EVALUATION

The scene performed was very effective and powerful for the audience. The actor playing Dysart and the actress playing Alan were very controlled. At the beginning, the actor playing Dysart paced up and down, slowly stepping one foot in front of the other, placing his heel to toe. This was executed almost in slow motion and it was extremely well controlled and mesmerising to watch. This action was taking place on the side of the stage symbolising 'society'. At the same time Dysart was saying, 'Take me'. This was significant as it showed how Dysart always puts himself under pressure and he feels guilty about taking away children's individuality.

The scene ended with a depiction of Dysart in the cage with Equus, which I think showed how by the end of the play Dysart is overpowered by Equus and Alan is free. Alan knelt in front of six candles and blew each one out, one by one. After each one, the actor arched their back and slowly outstretched their arms to the heavens, symbolising God being released from Alan. As each candle went out it reminded me of a funeral, maybe a funeral for the Equus (each horse represented by the candles) and Alan's worship.

When writing about an actor's performance, it is vital that you develop your writing skills to include adjectives that communicate how the actor moved, as well as saying what they were doing. This detail can help move your grades to the higher level.

EXPLORATIVE STRATEGIES

This unit is about using drama to explore a play text. The explorative strategies (see page 12) are drama techniques that can be employed to explore themes, ideas and characters from the play text. A key question for exploration here is 'what is normal?'

Work on your own in a space in the room. You are going to create two depictions and then thought track yourself finishing a sentence provided.

Prepare a depiction that shows 'normality' – a routine that everyone does (such as cleaning teeth, ironing clothes, reading the newspaper, staring at the television). Focus on your eyes and think about what Dysart describes as the dead stare, the moment when there is no passion inside an individual. Hold your depiction and finish the sentence:

- ■ I feel … (*or*)
- ■ I am …

Then prepare a depiction that shows Alan stood on the edge of his field of Ha Ha with Nugget behind him, or maybe feeding Nugget the sugar, or kneeling in front of the horse – a moment when Alan is consumed by Equus and feels passion. You need to communicate to your audience how he feels.

Hold your depiction and finish the sentence:

- ■ I feel …
- ■ I am …

Thinking questions

- ■ What is left of Alan at the end of the play?
- ■ Will he become easy to control now that he is passionless and has just joined the rat race?
- ■ If Dysart had not cut the passion out of Alan, what would Alan have become in the future?
- ■ What is Shaffer saying to his audience today?

Our job as actors is to place ourselves into the shoes of other people. This allows us to think about how other people feel from any time, place or context. Through this we may be able to know ourselves a little more, and we may be able to question what values inform society and what forces shape it. Drama allows us to examine human beings, and what makes us human.

Scene 34 is the climax of the play. The climax is the moment when the plot and sub-plot come together and are resolved. The build up in tension from the previous scenes reaches a climatic point. We bear witness to Alan Strang committing the crime we heard about in scene 2. All the episodes in the narrative have been leading to this one moment.

For your work on Unit 3 you may choose to work as a designer, and there are more details of that in the Unit 3 section of this guide.

Diegetic sound is sound that the characters on stage are aware of; a telephone ring, or a door slamming. **Non-diegetic** sound is sound heard by the audience that is not part of the world of the characters. Music underscoring a scene that is used to build tension for the audience is non-diegetic sound.

SCENE 34 –DESIGN ELEMENTS

Look at Scene 34 of *Equus*. Read it through, and imagine in your mind's eye what the visual, aural and spatial elements will look like on stage. Imagine the costumes, the horse's masks, the sound, the proxemics of the scene, the way vocal qualities are used and think about the lighting effects that you would use. Underline or highlight sentences from dialogue and from stage directions that give you clues about the drama elements you might employ.

Some selected extracts may be:

- A faint humming and drumming
- From the sides, horses converge
- The equus Noise is heard
- Dreadful creatures out of a nightmare
- Their eyes flare, their nostrils flare.

You are working as a designer on this scene. What is important for all design work is your ability to justify your decisions, to say why you have made the choices that you have. In any design work, you need to reflect upon the atmosphere and meaning the scene conveys and then discuss this with others to develop a design concept.

 Thinking questions

- What atmosphere is required for Scene 34?
- What meaning are you hoping to communicate to your audience?

A costume designer must analyse a character's social position, the period the play is set in, their characteristics and personality. A character's costume must communicate meaning to an audience. A set designer must create a three-dimensional space for the action of the play to take place in. They design the imaginative world of the play. Sound effects are used to create mood and atmosphere and to suggest period and setting. Sound can also be used to locate the action of a scene. Sound effects may include diegetic and non-diegetic elements.

Lighting design is used to create mood and atmosphere, essentially so the audience can see the action on stage. Colour plays a major part in the creation of atmosphere on stage.

Lighting is a relatively new dramatic element. Early Greek plays, right through to performances of Shakespeare text in the Elizabethan period were performed during the day to utilise the natural light of the sun. The first use of gaslights in the theatre was in the early 1800s and it wasn't until the 1880s that electric lights were introduced into the theatre.

A **gel** is a thin piece of coloured plastic sheet. The gel is placed just in front of the stage light to tint the light and produce a coloured beam. They are known as gels today because in the past they were made of gelatine.

Think tank

In any explorative work you are undertaking, it is always useful to think about the design elements, even if your teacher has not asked you to for that particular task. Think big and be inventive and then work to find practical solutions – to find ways of actually creating those effects. You may be lucky enough to have access to a full lighting rig and lighting-control board for each lesson, but if not there are other ways of creating atmosphere for a drama lesson. Torches offer you a narrow beam of light that can be focused on a given area or actor. They can act like a profile spot or a follow spot. An overhead projector with some gel placed over it can flood the stage with colour. They can act like a floodlight giving a general wash of light.

In any practical work, the health and safety aspects must be considered at all times. What are the risks in what we are doing and what precautions must be taken to avoid accidents or injury? To reach stage lighting we often have to use a tallescope or scaffolding tower. There are many health and safety aspects to think about when using these pieces of equipment and you must not attempt to climb them without your teacher's instruction. Lights should be screwed firmly in place on a lighting bar and have safety chains attached to them. If there is no safety chain the light should be removed. Any trailing cables must be taped up so that nothing can catch them and nobody will trip over them. You should always seek guidance from your teacher before you use any electrical equipment.

THEMES

Build a mood-board in response to this scene. A mood board is a collage of images, photographs, drawings and words that are your visual response to the scene. They are collected on an A3 piece of paper or card as a collage. You might also focus on textures and different types of material and stick these onto your mood board.

What are the major themes of scene 34?	What colour do you associate with that theme?	What effect do you hope to have on the audience?

What is the mood and atmosphere of scene 34?	What non-diegetic sound effects will support this mood?	Can you think of any songs that you might use to support this mood?

? Thinking questions

- What do the horses represent to Alan?
- Has this meaning changed since the first time he met them?
- How will you communicate this meaning to the audience through design elements? Think about the design of the horse's masks.

DRAMA ELEMENTS

Make a storyboard for scene 34 in six boxes. Focus on proxemics and semiotics, where actors are placed on stage in relation to each other. Under each box write down the lighting that will be used for that moment. Under each box write down any sound that will be used for that moment.

Lighting effects:
Sound effects:

Some useful websites that may give you inspiration:

- Society of British Theatre Designers: www.theatredesign.org.uk
- Association of Lighting Designers: www.ald.org.uk

Design a costume for Dysart for this scene. Design a costume for Alan to wear for the rest of the play. Annotate your costume designs. Say why you have made the decisions you have.

The Equus noise

Think about the Equus noise. Shaffer clearly defines what he believes the noise sounds like in his introduction to the text. The noise communicates to the audience the presence of Equus. The noise features heavily in scene 34.

Work with the whole class to make the Equus noise. Will you just use vocals in a soundscape or will you add noises created by other objects? What effect do you want to have on the audience? Think back to the effect Artaud wanted his work to have on his audience (see page 20 to 22).

If you can, record the Equus noise and play it through a sound-system.

COMMUNICATION

In pairs, you are to run a design meeting. One of you is to work in role as the designer and you are to present your design ideas:

- Your costume design
- Your storyboard
- Your lighting and sound ideas
- An idea for the set design.

Your partner will be the production's director. The director's job is to ask questions to ensure that the designer justifies all their ideas. Swap roles and repeat the exercise. Once you have both presented your ideas you are to reach a consensus on your design ideas and share this with the rest of the class.

KATIE MITCHELL

Katie Mitchell, a director who presents work all over the world and often at the National Theatre in London, says of design:

> 'The words of a play are just a guide as to what you are going to make; my craft as a theatre practitioner involves sound, light, physicality, visual imagery.'

Mitchell says when you first read a scene 'don't get caught up in the text as literature. Just read and picture the action in your mind.' Mitchell says that a good design 'will help an actor enter the imaginary world of this play in a concrete way. They will know the world of the play through the design. They will have a 360 degree understanding of the design.' Ultimately, Katie Mitchell says that 'mood, atmosphere, themes and action should be able to flourish and function within the design you create.'

Think tank

What we have done through analysing scene 34 using different drama mediums is to learn how to apply design elements to a play text. This is useful for anyone who is going to work as a designer for Unit 3, and it is also an important element for Unit 2. To gain top-band marks, you must be able to know how the application of drama mediums can enhance the communication of the meaning of a play text. Always think about design elements when you are preparing any drama work for an audience, then find a practical and simple way of achieving your ideas.

DOCUMENTARY RESPONSE

- You will write in detail about extracts that you studied closely and link them to the whole play
- You will explain how you used drama explorative strategies and mediums to explore the play's meanings, themes and issues

AN EVALUATION OF A LIVE PERFORMANCE

This will be an evaluation of a live production of the play that you have seen.

SENTENCE STARTERS

Below are some useful sentence starters to help guide you and help you write your very own documentary response. The answers are written by a GCSE candidate who achieved an A*. These are only selected extracts to help guide you and shape your own ideas and responses. This candidate studied *Equus* by Peter Shaffer.

> When I first read the play text, my initial response was …

When I first read the play my first thought was that Alan is very disturbed and that maybe he should be locked up. It is shocking when you first fully realise what Alan has done but, through investigation, you come to terms with *Equus* and Alan and actually realise why he does it. It is very poetic the way Dysart searches for his true self and how we see Alan lose faith in himself and society. Also as you investigate, through using drama, we understand more about Alan and now I'm sure if I read it again I wouldn't be angry or shocked by Alan but look more closely at the patterns of behaviour that lead up to the crime.

As you have learned in Unit 1, it is important you show your understanding of how a play deals with themes and issues. Have a look through the play text that you are studying and see what main themes you can identify are.

Two main themes and issues that came from studying the play *Equus* were:

Normality

A dictionary definition of 'normal' is 'conforming, adhering to, or constituting a usual or typical pattern, standard, level'. I think that you can't have an average personality. Everyone is individual and has their own personality. There isn't an average personality. Average means a common personality. How can there be commonality when everyone has their own personality? Normal can't simply be determined by these traits. This is why it is important in *Equus* that Shaffer, through characters such as Dysart, shows us that normality doesn't really exist.

Read how the candidate has clearly linked the definition from the dictionary to the play text and used examples of the characters to communicate to the examiner their thoughts and responses to an integral theme from the play.

> Developing your thinking
>
> Try to look at other plays the playwright you are studying has written and see if you can make any connections to the play you are studying now. Maybe you could research the world at the time the play was written and draw connections to the characters.

Worship

A dictionary definition of 'worship' is: 'the reverent love and allegiance accorded a deity, idol, or sacred object. A set of ceremonies, prayers or sacrifices made by religion or other forms by which love or adoration is expressed.' Worship in *Equus* is used to describe Alan's feelings towards Equus. He worships him, loves him and is loyal to him. Alan knows no boundaries in realising passion for the mysterious God. Worship and passion have a strong link. Worship can't exist without passion and passion wouldn't exist without worship.

Try to be analytical rather than descriptive.

Shaffer is clearly discussing normality versus extremity, mediocrity versus greatness in his play text. He examines worship and passion, belief and risk. I will now discuss what I believe *Equus* is about …

Shaffer writes about a 'decaying society' where a lot of themes show through the actions and character's speeches. Normality versus extremity refers to normal people versus extreme people, such as Alan, who are seen to worship an unknown, unusual thing. Extremity is where worship is taken to the limits, the place where Alan is with Equus. A quote about normality is found on page 63 where Dysart says to Hesther, 'you mean a normal boy has one head: a normal head has two ears?' Dysart questions a usual normal person saying this. He is being sarcastic towards Hesther. She says he has to restore Alan to 'a normal life'. Dysart can't understand what is normal. In another quote on page 65, Dysart again says: 'The normal is the good smile in a child's eyes — all right. It is also the dead stare in a million adults.'

Remember to always use quotes from the play to support the comments and reflections that you have made. The examiner may not know the play, so it is vital that you make it clear where the evidence is for your statements from the play.

The candidate has used an explorative strategy called layers of meaning. This is a drama explorative strategy that you can apply to any significant action. These five questions can ask to help you understand the reasons the character is acting out the action. Make sure that you choose a significant (meaningful) when you apply this explorative strategy in order to get the most meaningful answers.

Developing your thinking

Reading the meaning of the objects, action, sound, and lighting is a skill that you will develop and continue to develop as you progress through the course. It is important that you look not only at what you see but where it is placed on the stage in relationship to other objects. Think about the significance of placing an actor on one side of the stage in the position of a young child and, on the other far side, a small broken toy – this would read very differently to an actor sat centre-stage holding a broken toy.

Think tank

It is important that you quote from the text wisely. Try to select quotes that highlight the point that you are trying to communicate. The examiner will be impressed with your skill and ability to use quotes while explaining your point of view.

Throughout your study of Unit 1 and Unit 2, you will be using and exploring significant actions and objects. Here are some sentences that may help you start to communicate through your writing:

I feel the most significant piece of action in the whole unit of work was … Describe the moment in detail and say why you thought it was significant and what you learnt from it.

I feel the most significant action in the whole unit of work was Frank tearing the picture of Jesus down. I thought that this was the most significant action because it was a major turning point in Alan's life. Taking away his worship but then replacing it with another.

■ **My action** is taking away this picture, as I will not have my son being dictated to by a religion.

■ **My motivation** is the fact that I don't want his head full of hope when there isn't any.

■ **My investment** is that I get the knowledge that my son won't have to worry, he won't have pain in his life, and he will be left to grow on his own, like me.

■ **My model** is my father. He controlled me and I need to control Alan. This picture won't control him.

■ **The world for me is a place where** religion is control and control can easily be taken away. No one controls me.

Think tank

You are now well equipped with the skills to write clearly and confidently about the significant actions and objects that you have used during this unit. You know that writing your opinion, supported by research and factual information, will raise your mark.

STORYBOARD

Draw a storyboard of a scene that you have developed from working with an extract from the play. Remember to be detailed and use drama vocabulary.

You can investigate how and where the play that you are studying was first performed and investigate reviews of any past productions. It is important to keep referring to your thoughts and opinions on the set design and how you think it serves the actors and impacts on the audience.

See pages 6-8 of the design skills resouce pack on this book's product page (www.rhinegold. co.uk) to see more detail and exploration of the use of sound.

EXPLORING THE USE OF SOUND IN THE PLAY TEXT

Briefly outline how sound would be used in a production of *Equus*.

■ I think that the most significant object in the play was the horse bit, also known by Alan as the "chinkle chankle".

"And Aeckwus spoke out of his chinkle - chankle!" The final quote in the play.

"There is now, in my mouth, this sharp chain. And it never comes out." Dysart is as attached to worship as Alan.

This represents Alan's attachment to Equus. He even puts a pretend bit in his mouth to worship Equus. Significant symbol of his passion.

"I've never forgotten it. Chinkle - chankle."

"I looked up into his mouth ... There was this chain in it."

The sounds of metal clanging, horses' hooves, heavy breath, air rushing through the horse's nostrils, the humming of the Equus kind.

As you can see this candidate has chosen the horse as a main symbol that represents sound in the play text *Equus*. They have communicated through an image and annotation what they think is significant about the horse and have used quotes from the play.

We used a lot of sound in the overall scheme of *Equus* but more significantly in the stable scene. There were many ways in which we could use sound. One example is soundscape. We used humming in the first part of our scene at the beginning to show that this was a ritual to Equus. Equus was our God and we needed to show how much we would give to him. We started slowly humming quietly but then gradually built up the volume level. We also used sticks at the beginning as another ritual technique to build the tension and whipping sound. We consistently used the tapping of the sticks on a cage to show the pattern of ritual. We all carried on playing our part until our God reveals himself. The audience were quite shocked by the noise, as when we combined the sticks with humming and then the word 'Ek' being repeated it turned into more of a sacrificial sound rather than ritual. I liked the idea of a sacrifice because Alan does sacrifice his own old beliefs to be with Equus.

Developing your thinking

Notice that the candidate is writing about both abstract and naturalistic uses of sound. The description of how they as a group built up the sound collage is very clear – you could almost hear it. Look for the use of sound in your play text and experiment with how you could develop an atmosphere that may reflect the true feelings of the character, as well as the normal sound effects that may need to be in place.

EVALUATING AND CLOSING THOUGHTS

The examiner will want you to have reflected on your own work as well as that of your peers. In class it is very important that you record, in note form, your thoughts and reflections on someone else's work. Think how you would write to someone who was not present. How can you recapture the tension, excitement and well-crafted ideas? Overleaf are some suggested sentence starters that you may want to use to guide you through the final part of your documentary response.

Studying the play text I am beginning to understand how Shaffer viewed the society we lived in …

Studying this play has helped me understand that plays can hold a social message. This play was saying …

This unit has advanced my understanding of drama. I now understand …

The drama explorative strategies that I used well during this module were … because …

The drama mediums that I think worked well during this module were … because …

If we were to work on this play again, I would change some things. These would be … because …

If you find writing challenging, take advantage of using diagrams, charts, thought-bubbles, photographs and so on. The more creative you are, the more the examiner will benefit from reading your interpretation of the play text and themes you have been exploring.

Think tank

You now have the tools to write a detailed, concise and well-supported documentary response for both Unit 1 and Unit 2. The sentences above are generic and you can apply them easily to the work that you are carrying out in class. It is vital that you keep a record of work as you progress through each unit. You can refer to this when you have to compile all of your notes for your final documentary response.

Accurate spelling, punctuation and grammar are integral to you gaining a high grade, so get someone else to read through the notes that you are going to use in class. You can read a friends and they read yours and you will both be able to develop each other's work and you may suggest improvements. Be proud of your documentary response as it is performance in itself. Instead of standing on stage it is laying on a page waiting to be read.

RESPONSE TO A LIVE PERFORMANCE

The exam board says	What does it mean?
Write an evaluation of an experience of live theatre as a member of the audience.	We will focus on the word evaluation over the next few pages, but this word suggests you must discuss the value of the performance. You need to ask yourself: ■ What was it trying to do? ■ Did it do it well? ■ What could have been done differently?

Live theatre	This means being in an audience watching live performers performing a complete play on stage (not extracts or short scenes and not a performance that involves students). The performers could be amateurs or they could be professional performers. (This does not include performances on DVD/video.)
Maximum 2,000 words	This evaluation will be written in class, supervised by your teacher. You can make notes before you write your final evaluation and have them with you, but your teacher will supervise you writing your final draft.
Quality of written communication (QWC)	You will be assessed on the structure and presentation of your ideas and your work and grammar, punctuation and spelling. You will be marked on your response to the live performance and then your mark will be adjusted to reflect QWC, which includes: ■ Spelling ■ Punctuation ■ Grammar ■ Use of drama language.
The person marking this evaluation will look to see if there are judgements that are informed and justified.	You will need to make critical and informed opinions based on your own knowledge and your own reactions to the performance; all your responses must be balanced and considered, and you must work to avoid making extreme comments. You will always say why you think something and give an example from the production to back up what you are saying. P.E.E. on your work: P = make you point | E = give your evidence | E = evaluate the point This is what I think, this is the example from the production, this is how well it worked.

Think tank

Although you only submit one evaluation for your teacher to assess as part of Unit 2, it is sensible to practise your skills before you undertake the real evaluation. Watching a play on DVD can be a useful warm-up as you can pause the performance and discuss aspects of it and what notes you need to write down.

BEFORE YOUR VISIT TO THE THEATRE

It is useful to make some notes as you prepare for your theatre visit. Always remember you are going to see this production as a critical theatre practitioner, and you will be writing an evaluation of the performance when you return to your drama class room.

Remember to turn off your mobile phones and not to talk or whisper during the performance. Even on silent your mobile may interfere with the theatre's sound system. Watch the show and don't do anything that will disturb anyone else. Everyone in the audience has come to watch the show and they should be allowed to do this in peace. If you enjoy what you are watching this is easy. Some of you may sit back and let your concentration wander if you don't like what you are seeing, but that is really when your thinking as a developed theatre practitioner should kick in. Think about why you don't like the play and why it is not holding your attention. Look at the choices the director or the actors or the designers have made and think about what you would have done differently. It is sometimes easier to write about a piece of theatre if you didn't really like it because that way you are more critical and detached.

WHAT ARE YOUR EXPECTATIONS?

The company

Revise performance styles on page 19.

- Can you find any information about the company who are performing the show? What expectations does that information give you?
- What performance style does this company usually perform in?
- Do you know if this company uses the techniques of the different theatre practitioners?

Revise the practitioners on pages 20-27.

The theatre space

Revise theatre layouts on pages 28-32.

- Can you find any information about the theatre space you are going to watch this performance in? What type of performance layout does the theatre space have?

The playwright

- Have you done any research about the playwright? What is their work usually like?
- What expectations does this set up about the performance you are going to see?

The play text

- If it is an old play can you read sections of the text?
- What do you think are the key sections?
- How would you mark these moments if you were directing the play?

The advertising

- Look at the poster or leaflet image for the production. What information can you read from the signs given to you on the poster?
- What blurb is on the advertising? What expectations does this set up about the performance you are going to see?

Critical reviews

Prior to your theatre visit, read a variety of reviews about the show. You may end up disagreeing with what they say, but it will stimulate your thinking and give you some things to look out for when you watch the show.

Your teacher will help you decide what to write about before you finally write your evaluation for Unit 2. This will depend on what sort of production you have seen. Before then, you will need to write up your notes so you have them with you when you write up your review supervised by your teacher.

Produce a list of the following information:

■ The name of the play and playwright
■ The name of the company that put on the show, the theatre you saw it in and the date you saw it on
■ Note down the names of: director /designer/lighting director/sound designer/ cast and the roles that they played.

Background

■ When was the text written?
■ When was the first production and how was it received by the audience then?
■ Can you justify why anyone should stage this play today? Does it say anything about the way we live today?
■ What was the genre/style of the play text?

Structure

Provide a brief summary of the structure of the performance.

■ Was it divided into Acts or scenes? Was there an interval?
■ What was the setting for the play – does it change?
■ Was there a change of time or location in the play?
■ Did the company make use of multimedia? (projections/lighting effects/live music).

Plot

Tell the story of the play. This is a simple task, and you will not retell the story in your supervised evaluation, but what you will comment on is: the ideas or themes that emerge from the plot; was there a sub-plot going on?

Props/costumes

- What did the characters wear?
- Were the costumes symbolic or naturalistic?
- Did you notice anything about the colour of costumes? Was this significant?
- Is it possible to say which theatre practitioner has influenced this production?

Technical effects

How were effects used and did they create an appropriate atmosphere? Think about:

- Lighting
- Projection
- Blackouts
- Strobe machines
- Dry ice and smoke

As well as all the other technical effects the production employed.

Staging

- Comment on the set
- Draw small sketches to remind yourself of it.

Direction

- Was there anything that stood out and was effective in this production?
- Discuss three key moments and what choices the director had made when he staged those moments.

Acting/characterisation

Comment on the performances of individual actors and the way in which they related to one another: what was effective; and what could have been improved?

You have spent your course making decisions about which drama mediums, elements of drama and techniques to choose when you make your own drama. All you are being asked to do now is evaluate another practitioner's choices and discuss the value of the choices they have made.

UNIT 3 – DRAMA PERFORMANCE

This is your chance to show off all the skills that you have learned from Units 1 and 2. Unit 3 is a performance examination and is worth 40% of your final GCSE grade. That is a significant proportion of your overall grade, so make this a great performance. Skills that you will need to demonstrate are:

- Knowledge of practical drama skills through live performance
- Communication of meaning to your audience
- Working as a performer or a performance-support candidate.

This work is externally assessed and will take place between 1 February and 31 May at a date agreed by your teacher and the examiner. You must be in a group sized between 3 and 9 performers. The performance time should be no less than 15 minutes and no more than 45 minutes for larger groups; the examiner will stop marking if you are significantly over your time limit. You can offer scripted (see page 96), devised (see page 102) or a combination of both kinds of work (see page 109).

The areas you will be assessed on are:

Voice and movement   Roles and characterisation   Communication   Content   Style and form

ASSIGNMENT BRIEF

Your teacher will be sent an assignment brief and they will deliver lessons that will explore this brief. This means that the brief is there as a beginning stimuli rather than something you need to adhere and stick closely to. The brief will be broad enough for you to have relatively free reign. You will interpret the assignment brief with guidance from your teacher in one of three ways:

1. You can choose a script/published play that you think links in some way to the brief. You can then choose a section of this play, choose and learn the lines and stage your interpretation ready for a final presentation to a visiting examiner.

2. The second way you can interpret the brief is to choose a story of your choice and devise a play from that story. You may start with some song lyrics, pictures, significant objects or a theme to create a performance that will be performed and assessed by a visiting examiner.

3. You may wish to work on a hybrid form, where you devise and use a script. You choose a script that you want to use and adapt it by mixing the real text with your words.

Wherever possible get your peers to watch your performance as it is being created and encourage them to be critical and ask questions. When you think your piece is finished, film it and watch it back. Have the examination criteria that the examiner will be using to hand (ask your teacher for a copy) and while you watch use a highlighter to highlight what band you think your performance belongs in. Ask yourselves if you were the examiner what band you would award. What can you do to raise your standards before the examination?

HOW TO PREPARE FOR UNIT 3

Firstly, you need to make the choice of whether you would like to be assessed as a performer or as a performance-support candidate. It is important that you ask for guidance on making this decision from your teacher.

For performance support you can look at the design skills resource pack on this book's product page (www.rhinegold.co.uk) for more detail on what skills you will need to demonstrate. You will be working with a group and only one performance-support candidate is allowed per group. You must select from the following:

- Lighting
- Costume
- Sound
- Make-up/masks
- Setting/props.

You then need to choose whether you are going to produce a **scripted**, **devised or hybrid** performance. Once you have made these two significant choices, you are ready to embark upon the following advice.

ADVICE

This section of the book will take you through the skills you will use no matter whether you are using a script, devising or the hybrid format. The sections have been divided into scripted, devised and hybrid to help you navigate your way through. If you choose the performing option you will need to use the following skills and techniques on the following pages:

VOICE AND MOVEMENT

You will need to be able to show how you can match movement and voice to the characters that you perform. You will need to draw upon your experiences of what emotional qualities your character will need and what decisions you will make as an actor.

To extend your skills you can make sure that you are breathing correctly. If your shoulders go up and down when you are taking a deep breath, you are not getting very much air at all. When you breathe, your stomach should always come in and out. This is because, when you breathe correctly, you use your diaphragm, which is located just below your ribcage.

What the examiners are looking for in your vocal performance: To be awarded top-band marks the examiner is expecting: 'Vocal skills that demonstrate an outstanding use of pace, pitch, pause and tone.' To make sure that you are outstanding make careful decisions about how your character is speaking to the other characters. You will need to be sensitive to what your character's journey is throughout the play and what changes happen for them.

The style and genre that you choose to use for your performance will have a significant effect on how you fare in this area of the examination. You may choose a genre that demands large gestures and caricatures; therefore, you will need to perform in this style with conviction and skill. Or you may wish to draw upon your knowledge of Stanislavski and put together a performance that is fluent in narrative and demonstrates real life on stage. Make sure you pay careful attention to the areas of stillness in your performance together with carefully placed pauses. Remember to include in whatever style or genre that you choose clear facial expressions so that you are signing the correct clues to the audience and examiner.

What the examiners are looking for in your movement performance: In order to reach the top band, the examiner is expecting: 'Movement [that] demonstrates an outstanding use of gesture, stillness, fluency and expression.' To make sure that you are outstanding in movement, you will need to remain healthy, focused and prepared for your performance; like you would prepare for a sports event you should warm up your body and mind. Ask your drama teacher for guidance with these exercises.

Think about your use of:

PACE	The speed with which you deliver your dialogue
PAUSE	Moments of silence which could be filled with a significant cough or shuffle of your feet – a silent communication to the audience
GESTURE	Physical actions that communicate an understanding of the underlying messages or themes of your production
PROJECTION	Simply – can the audience hear you? Does projection change depending on what we are communicating?
MOVEMENT	Are there moments of physical theatre where you can express ideas and emotions without any words?
SOUNDSCAPES	Are there moments in your drama where you can create soundscapes with your voices?

ROLE AND CHARACTERISATION

Developing a role is a challenging task. You can do this in a variety of ways and your teacher will guide you with some exercises that will help. It is important that you look at the reasons and motivations behind the character and why they exist. If you are working with a script, the clues will be in the choice of language, length and amount of lines and how they communicate to other characters in the play. Start at the beginning of the play and map out your characters' significant mood changes in the script. What have you noticed about their emotional journey? How resilient are they to the challenges presented to them in the script? Are they the victim/perpetrator or both?

> What the examiner is looking for: 'There is an outstanding demonstration of the creation of role/character showing the complete commitment and imagination'. If you are devising and there is no script to investigate you may want to refer to the devising section from page 102.

Think about your use of:

PHYSICAL SKILLS	The way your character walks, stands or sits, their posture, the way they use stillness, the way they use gestures.
PSYCHO-TECHNIQUES	Revise Stanislavski on pages 23 to 24. This is the use of voice, language, expression and movement, using Stanislavski's system.
ROLE	This is the part an actor plays. Even in group work, think about your role and your character.
CHARACTERISATION	This is the choices you make as an actor; the way you use your voice and your body to represent the character you are playing.

COMMUNICATION

> What the examiner is looking for: 'There is outstanding communication with other performers, audience members and the visiting examiner.' In order for you to be outstanding, you will need to think about how you are defining your space and shaping your performance. Depending on what script or practitioner you choose to influence your performance, you will need to think about the actor/audience relationship.

Think about your use of:

COMMUNICATION WITH THE AUDIENCE	Your performance must communicate something to your audience. For this to be successful you as a performer must know what it is you are trying to communicate.
COMMUNICATION WITH YOUR FELLOW PERFORMERS	You are working as a member of a performance company – a team. You must work with them to communicate to your audience. You must connect with the other performers and know your role and how your character fits into what is being communicated to the audience.

CONTENT, STYLE AND FORM

Content reflects the narrative of your play and the issues, morals or questions it presents to your audience.

STYLE

This is the way your performance will look on stage. As you create, rehearse and perfect your piece, the style will become more refined and focused. The choice of practitioner that influences you the most will have a significant impact on how you are acting and shape of your performance will look.

FORM

This reflects the conventions of a particular time period in theatre. An example of this could be from Greek theatre, where they used the convention of the chorus, or Brechtian epic theatre, in which they used the conventions of breaking the fourth wall. The examiner will be looking for evidence of conventions that you have chosen to use in your drama.

Think about:

CONTENT	Think about the effect you want to have on your audience. Many practitioners such as Brecht and Artaud wanted to provoke their audience. Do you want to shock your audience, wake them up and move them outside of their comfort zones? You should consider your aims for your drama and that will help you decide on the content of your piece.
STYLE	This is about the way the actors perform. It is also to do with the choice of techniques and the choice of practitioners you may follow. You might employ a 'Brechtian style', other possibilities might include – total theatre, physical theatre, Expressionism or Naturalism. You might even decide to construct a piece of Theatre In Education to perform to other students in another school.
FORM	This is the shape and structure of your drama. Form refers not to what is communicated but how it is communicated. This is the use of the elements of drama. You must remember to experiment with form – all your rehearsals and devising sessions should be 75% practical, 25% discussion.

Be careful to choose subjects that you understand and that you have a clear justification for using the stimulus or script. If you are looking at performing a true story you will need to remain ethical and treat the subject matter with sensitivity and maturity. What impact are you wishing to have on your audience? If you wish to perform a comedy, a devised piece or a Shakespeare script, you will still need to understand fully what your intentions are for an audience.

THE LEAD UP TO YOUR EXAM

Remember this is a formal exam; it may be a practical exam rather than a written exam, but there is still an examiner and you need to create the right conditions to make sure you can get the best grades possible.

FINAL REHEARSALS

As the exam date approaches, make sure you timetable in a couple of full run-throughs of your piece. It is useful to have an outside eye at this stage. An outside eye is somebody who watches your piece and then gives you feedback. Your teacher may act as an outside eye, or you may ask one of your friends. Filming a final run through is useful as well; you can watch it back as a group and give each other notes and also watch your own performance.

> If there are three of you in a group, your performance should be around 15 minutes in length. If you are working in the maximum group size of nine then your piece should be around 45 minutes in length. Make sure your drama does not go over this time limit.

 Thinking questions

- Is your communication clear? Do you know what you are attempting to say to your audience?
- Do you have all your props and set? Do you know how they get on and off the stage? Have you rehearsed scene changes if there are to be any?
- Are you all clear on what costume you will be wearing? Make sure you do a final run-through in costume to make sure you can move properly in it and to make sure you can do all the movement that is required of you in your costume.
- Do you have someone who will be operating your sound and lighting? If not, have you rehearsed operating the sound and lighting for your piece?
- Have you thought about performing your piece to a critical audience? This audience may be the rest of your class, or some friends you perform for at lunchtime or after school. Have some set questions to ask them after the performance, questions that check on what is being communicated to them.

TECHNICAL REHEARSAL

Every drama classroom or studio will have different technical equipment, but it is vital that you rehearse in your performance space with any lighting and sound that you are using. If someone else is to operate your sound and lighting, then check they know where each cue comes. A cue is the line or the piece of stage action that a lighting or sound effect should occur on. Rehearse the cues to show your technical operators where each effect happens.

 Thinking questions

- Have you checked the level and volume of your sound effects? Have these been noted down?

- If a piece of music is playing underneath dialogue, have you checked the levels? Play the music and have the actor speaking over it to ensure that you have correctly balanced the sound and the vocals.
- Have you looked at your lighting effects? Does the lighting do what you want it to do? Nominate one of your cast to step out and have a look at each lighting cue to check it is as you imagined. Has the lighting been noted down or programmed into your lighting board?

DRESS REHEARSAL

This is a final run-though as if to a real audience for the exam. Remember you should never stop or come out of role as this will lose you marks. It is useful to film this final run through so you can watch it back and make any final alterations before the big day.

THE DAY OF THE EXAM

Remember this performance is worth 40% of your final mark for your drama GCSE. Prepare for it as you would for any other exam.

- Make sure your performance space is set up and ready for the exam. Is it as tidy as it can be?
- Ensure that you have an audience for your performance who will be supportive and who have been reminded that this is a practical exam and they need to behave appropriately.
- Help your teacher prepare for the exam. If the exam is happening during the day, have you made every effort to ensure your performance won't be disturbed? Help your teacher by making sure there are signs outside your drama space asking people to be silent because there is an exam in progress. Make sure there is a no entry sign on the door of your drama space.
- Help your teacher set up the examiner's desk; can you put a small light on the desk so the examiner can see to make notes? Make sure the examiner has the best view of your performance.
- Help your teacher by making sure the camera is set up. The camera must be in the second best position to record your performance for the exam board. Is there someone who knows how to operate the camera?
- Before the performance begins you will have to say your name and your candidate number to the camera. Make sure you know your candidate number at this point. You will also meet the examiner before the performance so they know who you are.
- Help the examiner by not all wearing the same clothes. If you are all dressed in black, how will the examiner know who you are?
- Before you perform make sure you have a cast warm-up. You can not expect to do well if you do not focus before the performance.
- Remember the examiner is looking to give you as many marks as they can for your performance. But, if you come out of role, if you laugh, or if you stop the performance then the examiner will take marks off.

This also applies if there is a technical mistake. If something goes wrong with the lights or the sound then you will not lose a mark as a performer if you stay in role and do not stop. You will lose marks if you stop or come out of role.

PERFORMANCE OF A SCRIPTED PLAY: BLOOD BROTHERS

Blood Brothers by Willy Russell (Methuen 2001).

In order to help guide you on how to use a script for your Unit 3 performance, we have chosen *Blood Brothers* by Willy Russell. This is one of the longest-running and most successful West End musicals. *Blood Brothers* premiered at the Liverpool Playhouse in January 1983. You can of course choose any script and it is encouraged that you find a script that not only challenges you and your peers but your audience too.

WORKING WITH A TEXT AND CREATING YOUR UNIT 3 PERFORMANCE

Step one will be to read the play. As you are reading, complete the table below to help keep what you have read in a format so that you can draw reference at a later stage. It is important for you to understand the plot, structure, shape and style so that you can interpret what the playwright is intending.

GIVENS (THE FACTS)

■ Twin brothers are separated at birth because their mother cannot afford to keep them both
■ She gives one of them away to wealthy Mrs Lyons and they grow up as friends in ignorance of them being brothers
■ Willy Russell's tale of two brothers considers class, fate and destiny, childhood and adolescence, surrogacy, superstition, humour and tragedy.

Character	Significant action	Page number/quote

Keeping a table like this will not only remind you of where the most tension, dramatic and memorable moments are but it will also teach you how to begin the process of analysing a text. After you have read the play it is a good idea to record your initial responses to the events and characters. These responses will help you and your peers decide which scenes you think would be the most powerful and have high impact for an audience.

Once you have read and understood the play, it is now time to select the section of script that you wish to perform. Each section must remain as it is written in the script but the way you stage the scenes is completely up to you and your peers.

REFINING YOUR CHOICE OF SCRIPT

Re-read the section(s) of script that you have chosen and try reading as if you are the characters. It is important that you all get a chance to read the different parts as you will all have slightly different interpretations of the character.

Think tank

Consider the drama explorative strategies that you will use:

- Still image (depiction)   Role-play   Forum theatre   Action narrating
- Thought-tracking   Layers of meaning   Context   Hot-seating
- Marking the moment   Significance of action
- Brechtian techniques - direct address, breaking the fourth wall, use of song and narrator

Consider the drama mediums that you will use:

- The existing structure and conventions of a play text
- The use of voice
- The use of spoken language
- Use of song and music
- Use of set/props
- Use of space/levels
- Devising and improvising techniques
- Use of set, costume and lighting.

ANALYSING AND WORKING WITH A SCRIPT

Breaking up the script: main themes

Reading Act 1 scene 1 of *Blood Brothers*, where the narrator sets the scene, you could split the lines between all of you so that all actors have a chance of performing. The examiner also sees you applying a choral, canon effect. The play includes rhyme-ballads and these can be performed directly to the audience as a distancing technique in scenes with high tension.

Thinking about the world of your play, how can this be depicted in your interpretation? For example, *Blood Brothers* is a play that shows both working-class and bourgeois (middle-class) England. These two opposing worlds can be signified in costume, props and accents. How will you get your audience to understand these two worlds?

DEVELOPING YOUR CHARACTER AND ROLE: ACTION YOUR TEXT

Stanislavski calls this units of action. It is important to recognise where in the script the narrative of characters' motivation has changed. Refer to pages 23 and 24.

One common error when working on Unit 3 is that you get restricted by the text and don't focus on the action. To avoid this, and to make sure you are working towards the-top band marks, you will need to go through the section of script and note where the significant turning points happen. After you have identified the turning points, you will now need to match them with actions. Try to signify to the audience what is happening in the story through action.

Think tank

Now you have employed the skills needed to read a script, analysing and identifying characters' turning points, you are now able to prepare action as well as text to communicate meaning to an audience. Remember the minute you go off-stage you are not being marked. Think about creating the images that are being talked about by the character on stage. Can you create still images in the background behind a back projection? Can you use placards to echo the social message of the play to the audience? Try to create, develop and devise exciting and original ideas to impress examiners.

Once you have discovered the deeper meanings, you can now return to the script and perform a more detailed and honest performance which will work towards your character and role assessment. In order to understand your character, you can read your sections of the script with only your characters' lines. Draw a chart that shows the significant points in the script where your character changes in thought or emotion. You and your peers can compare and see similarities and differences to help you gain an understanding of the characters' through-line (overall emotional journey in the play).

REHEARSAL TECHNIQUE: OFF-SCRIPT REHEARSAL

You can work without the scripts to deepen your understanding of what is happening in the action and between the characters. An example of this from *Blood Brothers* would be Act 1 scene 6. Read this scene and put the scripts aside. Re-enact this using your own words the moment that the pact between the two mothers is forged. Using the layers of meaning rubric:

- What is your action (what are you actually doing)?
- What is your motivation (why are you doing this)?
- What is your investment (what will you gain)?
- Who is your model (who and where have you seen this before)?
- What is your stance (what is the world for you)?

By asking these questions, you will be exploring the characters' motivations beneath the significant actions they are doing. In addition to this, you can also think about the following:

- Why does this narrative shock/not shock a 20th-century audience?
- Where is this action seen witnessed in the wider world?
- What other choices did Mrs Johnstone have?
- What other choices did Mrs Lyons have?

■ Are their differences in class having any effect on their actions?

Adolphe Appia was a pioneer in set designing and it would be good for you to challenge the naturalistic setting and try to present a more abstract and symbolic one: en.wikipedia.org/wiki/Adolphe_Appia

SETTING THE SCENE: SCENEOGRAPHY

You will need to show the audience the main significant signs from the play, even though you are performing extracts from the whole text. Write down a list of significant props and draw out where you think they could be on your stage. The setting should complement and work with the actions that you and your peers have decided to use. It is vital that you do not get carried away with visually stunning set design if it does not serve the play and its actors. Remember these top tips:

■ Use significant objects that are symbolic rather than full costume changes
■ Try to use simple set ideas that can be used to represent different locations. It is possible to perform a play with just chairs
■ Avoid performing scenes that could be performed for radio. Your examiner needs action to mark.

INTERPRETING YOUR SCRIPT: ESTABLISHING THE CONTEXT (TIME, DATE AND PLACE)

It is important that you also look at the playwright's intentions before you apply your own. If you work with the knowledge of what the playwright is trying to communicate, you can only advance and develop these concepts. Ask yourself the following to identify what other texts could be possibly linked to your play:

■ What is the main narrative? Does it relate or link to another text?
■ What was the world of the playwright like when they were writing the play?
■ How is the world of the playwright represented in the play?
■ What song lyrics would match the themes or events of the world of the play?
■ What other images can you find that link to the play?

Using *Blood Brothers* as an example, there are two other pieces of text that link with the main issues and themes that are being explored. A play written by Bertolt Brecht called *The Caucasian Chalk Circle*, which features a scene where a child is being torn between two women shows the ownership and right to mother a child, a central theme in Brecht's play and therefore relevant to the themes within *Blood Brothers*. The second text is from the Bible; the story of Cain and Abel. Two brothers kill each other after fighting over livestock and God's love. The killing of brothers links directly to the play *Blood Brothers* as both brothers die at the end of the play. Can you find any other texts that link to the play that you have chosen? Ask your teachers and see if they can point you in the right direction.

Once you have thought about the above you will have a more rounded and clearer understanding of what Willy Russell was intending for his audience. From this point forward you will be in a better position to interpret the script and make informed decisions about how you and your peers will present your play.

Understanding the relationships between your character and the others in the play is really important because the examiner will be looking for evidence of actors being able to relate to each other on the stage. For you to be able to this you really need to understand the relationships between the characters. Why not get your peers to create a character chart that shows their character journey and you can identify moments when other characters are at points of high and low emotion?

 Subtext is the underlying – often the truthful – meaning beneath the actual text. This is often the hidden message that the character is trying to hide. However, the audience need to understand that the character is hiding something from the other character.

LAYING OUT THE SCENE: UNDERSTANDING YOUR PROXEMICS

Use pieces of A3 paper labelled with the locations, entrances and exits and significant props. Lay them out on the floor and begin to work with your scripts in your hand. As you move across the paper, note where you are stood. Think about the spatial relationships between your character and the others in that scene.

COMPARISONS BETWEEN CHARACTERS

A lot of information about the character that you will be playing is already within the text – it is your job to find it! Go through the play and highlight what other characters say about your character. You will be able to build up a picture of how others see you in the play and this will help you interpret your character and play them with more believability. In addition to this you can go back through and highlight what you say about yourself to others. This again is another layer to your character. As you highlight you can write next to the relevant quote what characteristics it reflects in your personality. This is an invaluable technique to use when you are developing your performance for your role. Others in your group will also benefit as they will have been able to see what they say about others and this will highlight characteristics that they may never have identified.

LANGUAGE, DIALOGUE AND LEARNING LINES

The examiner will expect your performance to be rehearsed to a polished standard. Your teacher will organise an audience; this can be made up from your peers or invited. As you are working with a script you will have to learn the lines that you have chosen. This can be difficult but there are ways of learning, remembering and retaining the lines. Firstly, if when you are saying the line you know the subtext and you are applying the action and standing in the right place you will have these as signals to your memory and, therefore, it will be easier through rehearsal to remember your lines. Your character has been written by a playwright and it is important that you bring that character to life. You can only achieve this if you understand when to apply the pauses, thought-process time and attitude.

- Think about saying your lines in different situations to explore alternative deliveries: this will help you to learn the lines and hear them in alternative, abstract situations that will force you to think of the meaning.
- Record your lines onto your iPod and listen to them as you journey to school.
- Meet up for regular rehearsals where you complete speed runs and line runs. Try not to get into a habit of rehearsing them in one or more patterns. This can lead to you delivering the lines with little or no emotion and they will sound as if you are reciting them rather than believing in them.

STRUCTURE, SHAPE AND PLOT

You are in charge of the structure of your performance, as it would be impossible to perform the whole play for your performance. You can play the sections that you have chosen in chronological order (the order that reflects the original structure of the play) or you may wish to put the scenes that you have chosen in an order that forces the audience to see it as a flash back or flash forward. However you decide to tackle it, you need to be conscience of your desired impact on your audience.

The shape of your performance is of course dictated to a certain extent by the style of the writing and the content of the narrative. If it is sad and heart-wrenching story, I would not expect you to be using slapstick or comic style. The shape of your play should match the style and structure. If you jar these too much you are at risk of creating a performance that is full of techniques and not much substance.

SHAPE

Every play has a particular shape to it and that shape is defined by the style of writing, content of narrative and the elements of drama used to stage the production. Your shape that you create with your extracts will be created through your attention on the following:

- The use of space and levels – there are complex relationships between the central characters. You will need to think carefully about where the actors will stand in relation to the other characters.
- The use of gesture and movement – as you are choosing extracts to perform from the play you will be able to apply slow motion, moments of whole group still images and clear actions that communicate the deeper meanings.
- The use of voice – each actor will have the opportunity to present the character in the original accent. This is not a necessity but an opportunity. If you are able to perform in an accent, and you can sustain it throughout the character's emotional journey, it is recommended. The voice is very powerful when used correctly. It is important that you warm up your voice and keep it prepped for your performance.

PLOT

As you are working with a script, the plot is essential and you are not likely to change this. You must sign to the audience the main features of the plot as you have selected sections of the play. Make sure that you can sign enough for the audience to have a connection emotionally or mentally to the character and their events.

Think tank

Working with a script is challenging as you are taking someone else's words and ideas and interpreting them through your eyes. The experience and learning skills that you have acquired through this process you will gain transferable skills that you can use in any other subjects that require you to observe, reflect, develop and imagine.

EDUCATIONPHOTOS.CO.UK

A DEVISED PERFORMANCE

Devising your very own performance for Unit 3 is a scary but exciting thought. It is important that you look at the guidelines below to help you create a dynamic, innovative and original piece of drama that will have a dramatic impact on your audience.

WHERE TO BEGIN WHEN DEVISING?

You will need to use your time wisely and restrict your devising sessions with a focus and goal to achieve, otherwise you may waste the time discussing and not achieving your final product.

STIMULI: THE STARTING POINT

In Unit 1 you will have used different stimuli from your teacher to devise and create your own drama. This may have been pictures, poems, lyrics from a song, or a photograph. It is now your job to find what you would consider to be exciting, thought provoking and memorable stimuli to begin your devising process.

Think tank

Try to look beyond emotive images that are personal and seek images, texts or objects that could provoke a political, social or historical shift in an audience. Look to historical events, natural disasters, global crises and true events, and scripts that have been written to challenge and force your audience to reassess their understanding of the world in which they live. Try to avoid creating pieces that are predictable and simplistic. If you want to devise a piece of drama on a sensitive subject such as bullying, eating disorders or alcoholism then it is vital that you substantiate your piece with factual information to prevent them from becoming clichéd and performed for purely shock value. Remember you will be talking to an audience that may have experienced these sensitive issues.

One way of generating lots of different stimuli is to get everyone in your group to bring in something that is important to them. This could be a photograph of a family member on a memorable occasion, a locket from a grandparent, or tickets from a concert and so on. From these objects you can share your experiences and moments when they were given or experienced. Have one member of your group acting as a scribe so that the ideas you all begin to share can be loosely recorded for your initial preparation.

WISH LIST

Once you have decided which group you are working in, you will need to share ideas that are already in your head. You will all have some elements of drama that you have been impressed with and you will each need to share these initial wish-list thoughts. On a large A1 piece of paper, with a pen each write down as many elements that you would like to include in your final piece of drama. The list could include ideas that may never come to fruition but it gives each of you a chance to air these ideas.

It is worth timing this exercise as you will uncover more of your wishes under time pressure. Remember that all of you will need a pen in hand rather than having one person being scribe.

TAKING THE STIMULUS TO THE STAGE

Once you have all collated your objects, poems, letters, lockets and so on, you need to share your connections to the object. It is important that you have chosen a stimulus that you are comfortable sharing with your peers. You can share in a variety of ways but sitting in a circle and sharing and listening is an immediate and simple way of communicating your connection to the object.

The next step will be for each of you to write a list of words/themes/responses to what you have heard. The lists that you create will uncover lots of themes, issues and topics that will be of interest to you. You will enjoy this initial stage as you are able to put all of your ideas together. You now need to get prepared to refine, select and reject some of the ideas in order to create the one that will be close to your final work.

Once you have grouped your ideas by coloured highlighters, you will be able to easily identify the most common ideas. These may not be the ideas that you want to use but it is an excellent process for your group to go through to refine any ideas. The discussions that you have when you all connecting the ideas will spark off other ideas too.

Once you have selected the ideas that you want to explore for your Unit 3, divide jobs up between you to complete before you next meet. You may want to send someone off to research a particular issue while another could find factual information. Another member could interview other people that may be connected to some of the ideas you are exploring. Think about looking to other departments in your school that may be able to help. Often, what you are looking for to help you is closer than you think. Before rushing to the internet, research what is available in your school first. Fill in a sheet like the one below to keep a record of your decisions.

Unit 3 devising project - action plan

Company name ....

Working title ....

Group roles ....

Action	Name	How/where/what	(Internet, books)	Notes

Think about plays that you have seen before and what you liked about them in terms of narrative, structure and quality. Your Unit 3 project will need to emulate this quality. Think about the following:

- ◼ **The story**: you will need to develop your spider diagram by researching the issues, themes and topics that you have been discussing with your group. You will need to have integrity and remain truthful if you are choosing a sensitive and contentious issue to explore.
- ◼ **The audience**: think about what impact you want to have on your audience. How do you intend to create this impact for them? Will you have them in the round so that it is an intimate piece that they feel involved in or will you place them end-on so that they are looking in on the action?

Look at pages 28 to 32 for ways of staging your piece.

- ◼ **The props**: you can choose one significant object that encompasses the main message of your play rather than lot of props that may clutter the stage. If you are working with a designer, then you will need to have discussions with them about how you imagine the performance space to look. Try to think about using objects that are symbolic rather than ones that are naturalistic and there for a purpose. You can project images, text or photographs to help sign the play's message to your audience.
- ◼ **Characters**: all of you will need significant characters that enable you to show off various emotions and vocal qualities. It is not recommended that you have one central character and the rest are narrating the story.

- **Technical**: you are not marked on these skills if you are entering as a performer. You may be fortunate enough to have a performance-support candidate that is working closely with your group and, therefore, you will be able to express your ideas together with theirs. If you are all performers it is still recommended that you think about how lighting, sound, costume, make-up and set impact upon your play.
- **Form and style**: make sure that you list the forms that you are including in your drama, otherwise you can have a play that tells a very compelling narrative but you are not showing off your drama skills. Remember that the style is important and mixing styles is not highly recommended because it can make a play confusing.

Developing your thinking

During the early stages you may come up with some creative and exciting ideas. Try not to pin the play down too soon as you will miss out on the fun of exploring and discovering new ways of communicating to an audience.

SELECTING AND REJECTING TO CREATE YOUR PLAY

This is an important stage in the devising process and you need to make decisions on the following: the content; your structure; your chosen style; the shape; and finally the plot. These elements are what can be referred to as the skeleton of your drama. Take the inspiration from your highlighted spider diagram. Remember that not all your ideas can be used for this play

STRUCTURE

Think about what structure you want your play to be told through.

- There are different structures that will have a different impact on how your play will be portrayed to your audience.

Chronological

- This is where your play will have a beginning, middle and end. Each scene will need to have a transition that is smooth and carefully planned to keep the flow in order. Try to avoid blackouts for your transitions, if you are simply moving position on the stage or bringing set on and off. The audience are intelligent and they know that you are moving around in the dark.

Cyclical

- This is where you will start with a flashback to the end of the play; it will end with that same scene again. This is a powerful structure to use as the audience know the outcome so they are thinking about where emotion and morality

When you are selecting and rejecting ideas, group dynamics and patience will be tested. You and your peers will feel the level of tension raise as it is difficult to hear your ideas being rejected. However, you need to keep the play in focus and decide what is best for all of you that are being marked and the impact your play will have on the audience.

lie in the play. It is important that you return to the end scene in exactly the format that you presented it at the beginning to make this form work.

Flash forward

■ This is a structure that can help your ideas leap into areas that you may not have considered. This is where you would take the story/narrative at a given time in the future. It can be exciting to take an existing story, that a lot of people are familiar with, and launch your audience into the future.

Flash back

■ This is a commonly used technique that works well when you want to communicate to the audience potential reasons why the character is in the situation or scenario that you have shown. Often actors find it difficult to transition from a scene that is happening in present time to one that has happened in the past. Ways around this are: echo the last words that were said in the present scene ('I remember when …') and while this is being said the actors move into the positions ready for the flash back; you can use placards to communicate when and where you are flashbacking too; you can use direct address to awaken the audience; you can use soundscape that is atmospheric or lyric based.

Episodic

■ This is where you will create scenes that stand alone. They have no need to have a scene that comes before or after to make the scene make sense. This is a particularly Brechtian structure as it keeps the audience from being sucked into the world of the play away from the real world. Remember that your scenes once created can now be presented in any order as they each are independent from each other.

Montage

■ This is where you mix all of your scenes that you have created up and create new meaning from that performance. This is a really good technique to use when you are rehearsing your play for Unit 3. If it is stale and not exciting, try mapping out the story and cutting the map into a card sort. You can then put the scenes in any order (montage) and see what is created.

> Fairytales work very well in this structure. It would be effective to take a common fairytale and present the characters in their lives ten years from now. What would have happened to their world, relationships and, most importantly, how would the story that you know well (their past) have affected them in their adult lives?

Think tank

You are now ready to decide as a group what structure you think will work the best for your narrative. If you have the play in titles, and only a loose idea of the narrative, you can use a card sort to play out the different structures.

The story below has been divided into sections and put into small boxes. These can then be cut up and played out in any order. You can keep it chronological, and perform a series of still images, or you can put the end at the beginning and vice versa to create a cyclical structure. If you do not have a clear enough narrative, you can use a well-known fairytale, put it into the main sections according to the significant actions that occur and then cut it up. Lay these out on the floor and begin to play. There is an example set of cards on the following page for you to experiment with.

In Sudan, it's midnight. Mende is sat crying. It is 2004.	Mende escapes the house and runs to a petrol station where she meets her saviour.
The village is raided by the enemy. Mende is captured.	It's Britain, it's midnight. Mende is sat writing her story.
In London, it's early morning. Mende is nursing her wound in the garden shed.	Mende sits by her sister's side, witnessing her pain and blood loss.
In the kitchen, Mende is preparing lunch for her master.	The family hang out the blood-stained sheet for all the community to see.
A soldier pins Mende down and repeatedly rapes her.	Mende is hugged by another survivor at her book-signing event.

UNIT 3 DEVISING PROJECT - CHARACTER CHART

Name and age	Physicality	History/past	Current/ present (job, family situation etc)	Relationship with other characters	Political stance	Perception of death
Helen 30	Thin and bony, very sharp features with a pointed mouth.	Alcoholic parent and religious mother. Looked after younger siblings.	Expecting a child. Diagnosed with fatal disease.	The girlfriend and daughter.	Right wing, works in London office.	Fears it.

On the previous page is an example of a character chart that you may wish to complete with your peers when you are working in a small group. After completing this grid, you will understand the character that you have devised on a deeper level.

Developing your thinking

In order for you to develop a role that will have depth and meaning, you could use the above chart. Each member of the group should sit with you and all the characters that are in the play will need to be completed. The physicality of your character is important. You may not be able to communicate the actual physical look that you imagine in your head but in this chart you are encouraged to write or stick a picture of someone you think is most like the physical appearance of your character.

The history of your character is essentially created through your imagination. Think about past events that could cause the symptoms that your character has in the present. You may be playing a character with some emotional instability this could have come from a dysfunctional upbringing. In this section of the chart you could record significant events that have occurred in their lives and have left an impact.

The current situation is what your character will be playing in your play. It is their actual situation in the play that you are creating. Try to include as much detail as possible, even if you do not intend to communicate it to the audience. As long as you know what your character does on a daily basis you will be believable.

The relationship with others section is important for you and your peers to complete. What you think your character's relationships with others may not be what your peers think. This section will require you all to have a discussion about the feelings that each character has towards each other.

The section on political stance is a very difficult part to complete. You will need to think about your characters social and political views on the world in which they live. They may be liberal or they may be Conservative. For the political stance part of the chart it is really important that you investigate what the differences are between right-wing, left-wing or central political values. Knowing this about your character will help you create their text and belief in the play's world.

The final part of the chart could be considered a little abstract but it can help you create a character that has a deeper level. Ask yourself what your character would think about death. Would they fear it? Welcome it? Are they at risk of dying? Will they laugh at the thought of death?

DEVELOPING TEXT

The following exercises provide guidance to aid you in generating text for your Unit 3 devised performance.

SPEED WRITING

You may wish to use starting words that are more related to the themes and issues of your play so that your speed writing is related directly.

Collect a piece of paper and a pen and move into a space.

The rules are that you must keep writing on the paper even if it means you are repeating a word over and over again. Set the timer for two minutes. Using the following words as a starting point, begin writing.

■ God is … ■ Love is … ■ I hate …

Share some examples with your peers and see what material can be used for your performance.

DEVELOPING TEXT FURTHER

Begin by creating a list as long as you can over one minute around the starting words: I wish …

Try to include fantastical elements as well as more simple wishes. They may range from wishes that could never be achieved to one that is more simple and likely to be achieved.

Your lists can be from your characters point of view and you can work the wishes into a monologue that you can perform in your devised play.

Think tank

You now have some skills which you can use to develop text for your devised performance. You can refer to the scripts that you have read in the past if you want to formulate the text that you have created into a script format.

A HYBRID – SCRIPT EXTRACTS/DEVISED WORK: MACBETH

As you know for Unit 3, you can choose to work as a performer in a group with between three and nine performers in it. As a performer you can choose to work on a scripted performance (see page 96), a devised performance (see page 102) or a combination of both. The next few project pages will work towards a performance combining script and devised work. This production will be a hybrid, a performance combing two different elements.

A hybrid performance can give you a head start over a devised performance. It offers you the opportunity of taking a script that interests you and devising around it. You could choose several script extracts and devise the links; maybe you could take the script and set it in a new context; or maybe you could add in physical theatre elements to explore the scripted play's ideas and key themes.

MARKS

There are four aspects of performance that the examiner will assess you on:

Roles and characterisation

■ Choose a starting point text that has some strong dynamic characters in it that you can take on and develop yourselves. The process of developing a hybrid performance starts with the narrative of the original text but is then developed through the creation of character. Look to explore and then develop characters that firstly support and then subvert the story.

Voice and movement

■ You must ensure that in your hybrid performance you have moments of appropriate movement; use of stillness, use of gestures and use of voice to depict the roles or characters you are playing.

Communication

■ Make sure you find the truth in your starting point text, which means to understand the themes, key ideas and issues raised it. Find the key extracts in the starting point text that inspire you and the group. Make sure these key extracts inspire creativity and experimentation within your performance group.

Content, style, form

■ As you start building your hybrid, you will need to decide on a style for your performance. Will it be realist or non-realist? Will it follow the techniques of one specific theatre practitioner? Will you have an elaborate set or will you approach design in a minimalist way?

Ensure that all elements of your performance fit the chosen style.

A HYBRID PERFORMANCE

1	2	3	4	5
Pick the text that you are interested in exploring for your hybrid. Make sure that the whole group are inspired by this choice; you will be working on it for a long period of time and it needs to spark creativity and inspire everyone.	Read the whole play text a couple of times. It might be that you are working on a text you have already encountered on this course or another course at school. It might be a play text of a professional performance you have already seen.	Select the major themes and key ideas in the text. This is an important aspect of the communication criteria that the examiner assesses you on. What is this play attempting to say? What does this play tell us about our world today?	Begin to select the script extracts that you wish to work on at this stage. You may start by simply staging those script extracts and then finding a way to link them all together, devising scenes that advance the plot between extracts. You may use the extracts as starting points for more improvisation.	Begin the 'playing' process, improvise and use your imagination. Generate lots and lots of ideas, keep making notes of all of them as you play and improvise, but keep returning to the original narrative and keep returning to the key themes and ideas that you highlighted.

6	7	8	9	10
Begin to develop characters. You have the bonus of having some strong characters written for you in your starting-point text but you will also develop new characters to fit the new context you are exploring for your production. Maybe you are going to look at the narrative through the eyes of a new character or a character that is only briefly mentioned in the original text?	Begin to include physical ideas and movement-based work. It may be that you include a movement to music to develop the narrative between one script extract and another, or a dance theatre piece might be included at the start to set the location or build mood and atmosphere. Movement with strong evocative music could be used to explore the themes and key ideas at the start of the performance.	Begin pulling together all the elements you have created and start to look at the structure of your piece. What structure will serve your play the best? Will an episodic structure, built up of lots of short scenes all moving the narrative onwards be better than a couple of long developed scenes? Have you agreed on what style and genre your piece will be utilising? This has probably become clear during the playing/improvising section.	Show your piece to a critical audience. As soon as your piece is running, as soon as you can show it in some loose form, then work to get feedback. In the first instance you might do a run through in front of a camera so you can give yourselves feedback and criticism, but as soon as you can gather together a small critical audience who you will perform to, and who you will then question afterwards about the communication, what was clear, and what wasn't.	You must then leave yourself rehearsal time. It is always tempting to keep playing with your piece, to keep improvising, to keep trying new things out. But, as soon as you can, you need to stop the improvising, and begin rehearsing what you have. This is an important part of the process.

There are many theatre companies who work in this way. Recently both Kneehigh Theatre and Frantic Assembly have created what can be seen as hybrid performances, performances that take a script as a starting point, use elements and extracts of the script but also include improvisation and the companies' own devised elements to make very successful shows. Each of these companies has very good websites that would be worth taking a look at.

HYBRID INSPIRED BY SHAKESPEARE'S MACBETH

Macbeth was written in 1606. James I was on the throne; before James Elizabeth I was on the throne. Under their rule England had changed from a Catholic country to a Protestant one, and this had proved to be a difficult process. James had recently been the target of the Catholic-led gunpowder plot. An attack on a monarch was believed by many at the time to be the greatest crime on earth, as under the divine right of kings, the monarch was assumed to be God's representative on earth. King James was also fascinated by witchcraft and even published a book on it; we must remember that members of society believed totally in the existence of witches. It is against such a background that the story of Macbeth's rise to power was written and performed for the first time.

DOUGLAS MCBRIDE

Macbeth and ghosts

DOUGLAS MCBRIDE

Macbeth and Lady Macbeth

DOUGLAS MCBRIDE

THE STORY

With any play that you are working on for performance, make sure you read it a couple of times through. You may find this text hard to read from cover to cover, and you may choose to just focus on understanding key scenes. Summaries of the story of *Macbeth* can easily be found online, see www.sparknotes.com/shakespeare, for example.

The main question to ask yourself is: what does this play have to say to us in our world today? This will become your first key idea and it is this idea that you will take into performance.

DEVELOPMENT QUESTIONS

- Would Macbeth make a good leader?
- Does Macbeth's past as a warlord stand him in good stead to lead a country?
- How will this affect him as a leader?
- At the start of the play Scotland is at war. How does being at war affect a country and the people living in it? Does it have any effect on them?
- What happens to a country when a leader misuses their power over their people?
- It is often said that it is children who are most affected by adults' mistakes. Could the whole performance be seen through the eyes of children who are acting out parts of the story as they hear them?
- Could the whole performance be seen through the eyes of the citizens, the normal people who live under a corrupt monarch? Your performance could show the effect major significant moments from the narrative have on them.

There are some strong characters in the text that will open up areas for discussion and thought:

The witches	Three old crones foretell the future to Macbeth. How will you choose to stage this element in your hybrid production? Do their words appear in a newspaper column as the character's horoscope, telling them what will happen in the week ahead? Do they appear to the characters in some strange way, maybe on a television screen, or by strange email or mobile-phone messages? Maybe they are just voices in the character's head, urging them to commit crimes?
King Duncan	In the original text he is the King of Scotland, a good and fair king. In your hybrid performance, you may change the context. Maybe Duncan is the head of a large corporation, or maybe the head of a record label or talent agency?
Macbeth	There are many questions that you could explore with this character and many links you could make with our world today. Macbeth becomes a leader, but does he make a good leader? What happens to an organisation or a country when you have a corrupt leader?
Lady Macbeth	You need to decide what she wants. What are her motivations? Does she want fame and power for herself or for her husband? What motivates Lady Macbeth to commit the crimes she does, and to urge Macbeth to do the evil deeds that he commits? Does she hear voices in her head? What makes her loose her mind at the end of the play? There are questions in the play about her child. Did she have a child but lost it at a young age, or is she unable to have children? Do these influences motivate Lady Macbeth?

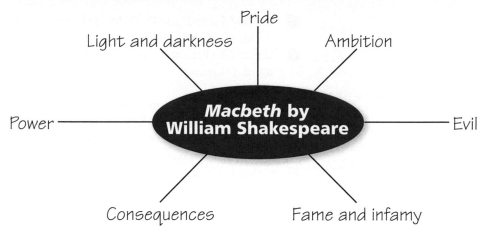

There are many themes in the play. These are just some suggestions that could fit an assignment brief from the exam board. A very quick practical way to start developing physical work is to:

■ Create depictions or action depictions of your key themes
■ Work on your transitions – the way you move between depiction to depiction
■ You could then run the sequence to music. This could be developed into a piece of physical theatre with short extracts from the text added to it, or recorded and mixed with the music by a sound designer.

Think about your key themes and ideas carefully. The way you communicate these is an important part of your assessment.

PRACTICAL EXPLORATION OF THEMES

Grandmothers' footsteps

You may know this game by another name. Play the game normally at first to remind yourself of the rules to this simple children's game. One person stands at the end of your drama space – they are 'grandma'. The rest of the class are at the opposite end. When grandma's back is turned, you creep forward silently. When grandma turns you must freeze. If grandma sees you move, you are out.

The second time around, grandmother becomes a king - if you are spotted, then you must give an excuse as to why you were moving towards the king. An excuse might be: 'I was bringing you a present' or 'I was coming to warn you of attack.' If the king believes your excuse, he will let you stay in, if not he will pull you out of the game. You might then replay the game exploring other characters as grandmother, and you responding to them in different roles.

While you work through all these practical exercises ensure that you have an outside eye – someone who is watching the practical work that you produce and making notes about the characters you begin to create, the narratives you begin to explore and the dialogue that you use. These will all be useful as you come to work on your hybrid performance. You could film all your practical work and sit down as a group after each exercise to make notes.

There are many websites where you can access the entire text of Shakespeare's *Macbeth* if you don't have a copy of the play:

- shakespeare.mit.edu/macbeth/full.html
- www.william-shakespeare.info/script-text-macbeth.htm

DEVELOPMENT QUESTIONS

- Could Macbeth and Lady Macbeth be working in a big business and they kill the chief executive in order to own the company?
- Could Macbeth and Lady Macbeth seek fame and celebrity so much they murder their way to the top?

Link extracts from the text to a new context. Look at the first scene of the play. This is when we first meet the three witches. Take just the words from the text and see if you can put the scene in a different context. Maybe the three witches work in an office, appear on television screens, appear in the mirrors that Lady Macbeth poses in during her preparation for fame. Putting a piece of text into a new context will give you new ideas for performance work.

Read the opening of the play from 'When shall we three meet again' to 'Hover through the fog and filthy air.'

DEVELOPMENT QUESTIONS

- Who are the three witches and what do they represent?
- How will you represent the witches using visual, aural, spatial elements?
- Do the witches ever actually appear or could they just be voices in the Macbeth's heads that give them excuse and reason to commit the terrible crimes that they commit in order to gain power and fame?

If any hybrid you work on, remember you don't have to accept the original setting characters are presented in. New contexts will help you communicate new ideas to your audience.

DEVELOP A NEW CONTEXT

Try improvising a scene as children. You live in Scotland, and you have heard about the brave soldier Macbeth and how he won the war for King Duncan. You have heard of the final battle when Macbeth ran through the enemy with a gleaming sword and plunged it into the leader of the enemy army and cut his stomach.

Read Act 1 scene 2 of the play from 'For brave Macbeth' to 'And fix'd his head upon our battlements.'

Prepare your scene which must include:

- Shakespeare's words from the text (above)
- The children acting out the battle
- The children sharing with each other their view of brave Macbeth.

DEVELOPING CHARACTERS – LADY MACBETH

Remember it is important that you develop strong characters who communicate meaning to an audience. As a performer you are aiming to become the role and communicate it with vocal skills, and by using appropriate movement. Your performance skills should be used to create a convincing character. The character you create should be totally believable to your audience (and your examiner) and you should remain in role throughout.

Write the letter that Macbeth writes to his wife. Decide on the context of the letter. Macbeth has just been promoted but to what position? Macbeth has just met the three witches. Have someone read the letter and have an actor centre-stage playing Lady Macbeth. The pupil in role must show Lady Macbeth's reactions physically as she realises the implications of the letter - that Duncan must be murdered and that she will join her husband at the top. Show the reactions in her face and hands particularly.

What does she do with the letter as she finishes reading ? To develop this scene you could include the Artaudian concept of revealing the double (see pages 20-22). What could Lady Macbeth's double reveal during the letter reading? Finish the scene with Macbeth entering and use the original Shakespearian text:

Read Act 1 scene 5 of the play from 'Thy letters have transported me beyond' (Lady Macbeth) to 'May read strange matters' (Lady Macbeth).

DEVELOPMENT QUESTIONS

■ Who needs the power and fame more, Macbeth or Lady Macbeth?
■ Who has more power in the relationship?

DEVELOPING CHARACTERS – MACBETH

Remember it is important that you develop strong characters who communicate meaning to an audience. Focus practically on the first moment Macbeth meets the witches on his way back from battle with Banquo. After the battle is won, Macbeth and Banquo – his friend - are returning home when they are confronted by three witches who speak to them:

Read Act 1 scene 3 of the play from 'Hail Macbeth, Thane of Glamis' (First witch) to '… that shall be King hereafter' (Second witch).

They then hand Macbeth a crown. They hold it in front of him, and when he takes it, it immediately disappears.

Dramatise this meeting, including the moment when the witches hand Macbeth a crown, which vanishes in his hands. Think about how the witches will appear to the two men. Research what type of woman would have been accused as being a witch during the time period the original text was written. Will the results of your research influence how your portray the witches? What will the two men's immediate reaction be? How do the women speak the three lines? What are the two men's reactions to these words and do they have different responses? Mark the moment that Macbeth is handed the crown. The crown is a signifier – what is the signified of this significant object? If you place the narrative in a different context, what object might you hand Macbeth? What clothing will Duncan be wearing? Focus on what meanings are being expressed through the elements of drama.

DEVELOPMENT QUESTIONS

What is important for your development of this hybrid performance is the context you have placed Macbeth and Lady Macbeth into. Think about props that are appropriate for this context and use them throughout your performance.

MARK THE MOMENT THAT MACBETH KILLS KING DUNCAN

Remember who King Duncan represents in the original context of this drama. Macbeth is not just killing the king, he is also killing a representative of God on earth. Link this to the narrative. Lady Macbeth drugs the servants' drinks so that they fall into a deep sleep. Macbeth takes their daggers from them to kill Duncan. Macbeth is to smear the two servants with Duncan's blood once he has been killed and replace their daggers. As Macbeth approaches King Duncan's bed-chamber he sees before him an invisble dagger and says:

Read Act 2 scene 1 from 'Is this a dagger…' to '… a false creation' (Macbeth).

Try and use parts of this extract, or the whole extract in your performance work. As a performance company set up:

- Duncan's bedchamber
- The outer room
- The two guards
- Macbeth, Lady Macbeth and Duncan

Use the drama mediums and work with tension and silence. The servants in your castle may wake at any minute. Duncan's guards may wake at any minute. Lady Macbeth is watching. Macbeth knows he is going against God's wishes. Macbeth knows that the guilt from this act will mean he will not sleep properly ever again because of the dreams and nightmares that will play on him.

Show Macbeth's long walk into and through the servants' chamber to Duncan. You could use the explorative strategy of narration here, with the rest of your performance company narating Macbeth's walk to murder.

You could use the explorative strategy of thought-tracking here to speak out loud the thoughts that are going through Macbeth's head as he approaches Duncan ready to murder him. You could use the explorative strategy of cross-cutting here to show what Scotland is like under Duncan's rule. You might show children living under Duncan's rule, a rule that is kind and fair and just, and cross cut to what the world will become under Macbeth's rule, a rule that is unkind, unfair and unjust. Add in the some tension as Macbeth passes a cross on the wall – what does he do at this moment? Could the cross speak to him?

Think about the chain of events that occur the next morning:

1. There is a knocking at the castle gates. It is Duncan's son with MacDuff and the gate is opened by the porter

2. The King's son MacDuff is taken to the King's bedroom

3. MacDuff finds Duncan dead

4. A meeting is immediately called.

Mark the each moment. What would Macbeth's response would be to each moment from the narrative? As a group, prepare an action depiction or a still image representing each of these moments. Macbeth stands outside of each of these still images. He could speak and finish the rubric:

A = My eyes or ears tell me (the social – Stanislavski's outer)

B = My head or heart tells me (the personal – Stanislavski's inner)

BANQUO'S GHOST

Macbeth and Lady Macbeth hold a banquet to which the ghost of Banquo's ghost attends to haunt Macbeth:

Read Act 3 scene 4 from 'Prithee, see there!' to 'Shall be the maws of kites' (Macbeth).

It is sometime easier to develop your understanding of a scene if you put it into your own words and develop an action narration. Below is an action narration text that takes the significant action of Act 3 scene 4 and puts in into contemporary language. You could do this for any significant scene in the play.

We are in the banqueting room in the castle. It is cold, and dark – lit only by candlelight. There is a breeze in the room and the candles flicker – struggling to stay alight. On one wall hangs a large wooden cross; opposite on another wall hangs the flag of Scotland. In the third wall is the entrance to the room. Placed under the wooden cross is a large wooden top-table with two chairs. In a semi-circle facing this table are other smaller tables and chairs. Three Thanes walk into the room, one behind the other - two of them take their places in the semi circle. The third stands in front of the top chair, touches it slowly, looks at the Scottish flag, shakes his head and then stands by the cross and crosses himself. A shout is heard – the King approaches. The other two Thanes turn and look behind them

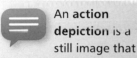

Developing your thinking

The porter has a very funny monologue in Act 2 scene 3 that he performs and this would be an excellent choice of monologue to perform if you are looking to develop your contribution to the performance or you are looking for a speech to perform for an audition. Make sure you break the speech into units of action.

An **action depiction** is a still image that includes a moment of action before the final freeze. As an actor you will show the ten seconds of action that lead up to the final freeze.

quickly, placing their hands on their swords, which are strapped to their belts. Lady Macbeth enters first; she walks into the room and stands still looking at the three Thanes. She waits and there is a pause. Slowly the Thanes bow their heads to her, and she takes her seat. Another pause. Macbeth then runs into the room and sits straight down. He whispers to Lady Macbeth.

Lady Macbeth   My husband feels a little un-well – he is sorry for being late – please sit.

The Thanes sit. Immediately Macbeth stands up and stares towards the entrance. He points.

Macbeth   Look, look – why are you here?

Lady Macbeth looks at her guests nervously and quickly.

Lady Macbeth   We invited all the Thanes my dearest.

She almost pushed her husband back into his seat. Macbeth jumps up again.

Macbeth   My cup – it moved – who has moved my cup?

He then moves towards the Thanes looking just above their heads.

Lady Macbeth   As I said, my husband is unwell, I apologies.

The Thanes whisper to each other. One of the Thanes looks towards the Scottish flag. Macbeth stares at the cross.

Macbeth   Why do you do this to me? Why are you here?

He crosses himself and then repeats this action three or four times. Lady Macbeth then moves over to the Thanes and begins pouring them wine.

Lady Macbeth   Drink, drink –please, and enjoy.

Macbeth then shouts out NO and stares at the seat where Lady Macbeth was sitting.

Macbeth   Get out, get out – you're not invited – leave now – get out.

Lady Macbeth, making her way over to hold her husband:

Lady Macbeth   My husband really is ill – I suggest you all go now.

Macbeth then runs towards the entrance.

Macbeth   Get out get out – leave me in peace – leave me in peace.

It is often said that reactions are much more important than a character's actions and good reactions bring about clear communication with your audience. Focus on what you do on stage when you are not speaking and when you are just listening and reacting. Let the words carry meaning in your dialogue. Let your physicality communicate meaning when you are reacting.

He leaves the room, quickly followed by Lady Macbeth. The Thanes leave the room whispering to each other in a group. Dramatise the scene firstly without somebody playing the part of the ghost – it is brought to life through Macbeth's actions only. Then repeat the scene with someone playing the part of the ghost. Focus on the **reactions** of the nobles and Macbeth's queen. The way they behave is crucial in supporting the illusion that Macbeth is able (or thinks he is able) to see some horrific sight. In both dramatisations, attention must be paid to how the tension is built and sustained. In both dramatisations Macbeth's and his queen's last actions are potentially significant. Reflect on the two versions assessing what the physical presence or not of the ghost offered by way of potential comunication of meaning. Which scene is the most effective dramatically?

Think tank

What you have worked through during the last few pages is how to start work on a hybrid performance. A hybrid performance is a performance that you construct using extracts of script and devised elements combined together. If you find it hard to start thinking of ideas when you are just devising, and struggle to come up with characters and narrative ideas, then a hybrid performance may suit your group better. You may find working on a script too restrictive. You may get frustrated because you want to add new scenes and new characters. You may want to focus on just one key theme or just one character. If this is the case then a hybrid performance may be the best way of working for you. The exercises and ideas presented over the last few pages are not just ideas to explore the play *Macbeth*. They are starting point ideas and exercises you could apply to any text.

THE ROLE OF THE DESIGNER

For the design skills resource pack that accompanies these pages, please refer to the downloadable pdfs of supporting material available on this book's product page on the Rhinegold website: www.rhinegold.co.uk. Here you will find details of the exam requirements for each design option, and ideas to lead you through each specific skill.

Omaha Community Playhouse, Omaha, Nebraska

STEVE BROSS

"Students can present their work as a performance-support student (a designer) in a single performance to an examiner." Pages 31 and 32 of the Edexcel GCSE specification.

Being a designer for Unit 3 should be an active choice. A choice made because you are passionate about the area of design you take on, not a choice made because you don't want to perform or you don't like the play the group are working on.

You can choose to work as a designer in the following areas, each of which is covered in detail in the design skills resource pack:

■ Lighting   ■ Costume   ■ Sound   ■ Masks/make-up   ■ Setting/props

Omaha Community Playhouse,
Omaha, Nebraska

The role of performance support is a difficult role to perform. You will work much more independently than the other students who are working as performers. You will need to attend all rehearsals, but you will also be expected to work on your own, researching, preparing all the written-support work, and building up your knowledge of your chosen skill. The positive element is that not only will you be marked on your contribution to the final performance but, unlike the performers themselves, you will have five minutes to talk to the examiner explaining your choices and processes.

WHAT DOES A DESIGNER DO?

The designer works with the director to realise their visual interpretation of the play. You will need to ask specific questions and then find a way to communicate your answers either visually or aurally, depending on your chosen skill.

Context	⟶	When is the play set, and how will you communicate this context to the audience?
Social context	⟶	What will your design communicate to the audience about the character's class and social standing?
The space	⟶	What is the layout of your performance space (revise pages 28 – 32) and how will this affect your design decisions?

The genre	⟶	What is the genre (the type of play) of the text you are working on and what elements does this mean you must include?
Theme and ideas	⟶	What are the central themes and ideas in this play? Have you agreed these with your director and cast? How will you reflect these ideas and themes in your design work?
Mood and atmosphere	⟶	Design creates mood and atmosphere. What mood and atmosphere does the play text need and what mood and atmosphere does your director require?
Practitioner	⟶	What practitioner's techniques will the play use and how will this affect your design decisions?

The resources your school has may dictate your design ideas. What set pieces, props and costumes does your drama department have that you can utilise and use in your design? Is there a budget for this production; are you the only play that will be performed on exam day or will you have to work around other groups? These are all questions you need to ask yourself and your teacher before you make any design decisions.

HOW WILL I BE MARKED AS A DESIGNER?

Web link

www.

Edexcel website:
www.edexcel.com/gcse2009

The Edexcel specification will give you further details about the documentation you need to produce for the examiner for each of the chosen skills. Make sure you are aware of what written work and design work you have to produce. Remember this is a minimum requirement.

Whichever option you choose you will have to complete the following tasks:

What is required of you	Tick if you think you have completed this
You are required to work collaboratively with all other group members	
Have you discussed your ideas with your director?	
Have you discussed your ideas with the cast?	
You are required to take advice, guidance and direction from the teacher	
Your design must work for the whole production, and your teacher as director will have an overview of this. Your design must enhance the performance not work against it. Have you taken advice from your teacher/director?	

You are required to communicate your chosen skill to an audience and to the examiner	
Have you agreed with your director and your actors on the key themes and ideas that the production is attempting to communicate?	
Have you found ways to reflect these key themes and ideas in your design?	
Have you included research ideas about these key themes in your written evidence?	
Have you completed a mood board to further explore these key themes and ideas?	

Give a presentation of no more than five minutes to the examiner	
Have you prepared all your research and support notes and presented them in a folder, on paper or on card?	
Have you thought about preparing a PowerPoint presentation to accompany your talk with the examiner? This will also show off your ICT skills.	
In your presentation do you show the examiner some lighting states, play some sound effects or show some costumes or props?	
Have you rehearsed your presentation?	
Do you include in your presentation ideas that you had and that you then rejected?	
Have you told the examiner key areas of your design that you wish them to focus on as they watch the performance?	

THE PRESENTATION

You have the chance to present to the examiner your ideas and your process. Rehearse your presentation, film it and watch it back just like the performers will. Using a PowerPoint presentation will keep you focused and will make your work look professional and organised. Have your portfolio and supporting notes laid out for the examiner to see. The aim is to tell the examiner key areas of your design that you want them to focus on during the performance.

One outline could be:

- Introduce the play and the key themes and ideas that you have chosen to focus on
- Show your research into these themes and ideas
- Discuss your theatre space and the impact that had on your design
- Discuss the givens from the text and the production – the facts that you couldn't argue with and had to support in your design; this will include, for example, the setting, the location, and the time of day
- Outline and explain all your design ideas
- Discuss your choices - what didn't make it into production? Explain why
- Show off your design, either by bringing up some lighting states or bringing in examples of your final design work
- Finish by telling the examiner the overall effect you are hoping to achieve with your design.

You will be marked under four separate grade criteria headings:

1. Justification of design decisions

- ■ Your design must fit the context of the performance
- ■ Your examiner will see this in your presentation and in performance
- ■ Does your design support the form and the genre of the production?

2. Documentation

- ■ The examiner will look at all your written support material. Make sure you draw their attention to all your work in your presentation. Make sure you reference your documentation.
- ■ There has to be some high quality design work here. Remember, different skills ask for different documentary material. Make sure you know what you have to produce, produce that and then more.

3. Realisation of design

- ■ Essentially you need to design to an outstanding standard and then fulfil that design to an outstanding standard.

4. Communication of design in performance

- ■ Your design must support the key themes and ideas of the production. It must be clear that direction, design, performance are all working together to support the director's concept for this production.
- ■ Your design must increase the quality of the performance. Without your design the performance would be weaker.

To assess your learning throughout your GCSE Drama course, please download the Subject Knowledge Audit grid as a pdf from this book's product page on the Rhinegold website: www.rhinegold.co.uk

Documentary response. This is the written work that you produce for Unit 1 (2,000 words) and Unit 2 (1,000 words). This work will be written up in controlled conditions, which means it is supervised by your teacher, and will tell the examiner about the process you have been through for each unit. It will reflect on your own work and the work of other people in your class. In the documentary response, you will evaluate the work you have completed, you will discuss and evaluate the way you presented your drama and the techniques you used.

Drama medium. The drama mediums are the techniques that we usually think about when we move into performance and theatre. Our dramas in the classroom help us to explore themes, issues and the bigger questions. When we move to perform those dramas to an audience we look to the drama medium as a way of enhancing the communication of the meaning to our audience.

Explorative strategies. These are techniques that you will use to reflect upon and deepen your understanding of your drama. They will help you develop your understanding about characters, the themes you are exploring and the questions you are asking. You will need to evaluate how each strategy helped you gain greater insight into your enquiry.

Expressionism. Expressionism is a movement in art and literature that seeks to communicate feelings rather than represent objects realistically. Expressionism sought to get rid of ideas about reality and explore the deeper meanings found underneath.

Forum theatre. As an audience member you make up the forum – the audience that is watching a piece of theatre. When you think you could change the action or react differently you say freeze and then step into a role taking the place of another actor. So, the group watching can enter the scene as any character or they can stop a scene and take over a role.

Gesture. Part of the semiotics of theatre, a gesture is a movement of a part of the body, especially a hand or the head that conveys meaning or an idea to an audience.

Hot-seating. As an actor you work in role and answer questions about yourself. Hot-seating helps to build up information about a role. What is important for you as an actor is to be in role when you answer the questions rather than just telling your audience the answers from the character's point of view. When you are being that character, for example, there may be some questions you refuse to answer.

Marking the moment. Marking the moment is a convention used to sign to the audience a significant moment in the drama. You could use drama strategies like freeze-framing or narration or you might employ drama mediums like spotlighting, use of sound effects, musical underscoring, or a change in the lighting.

Model box. A model box is a scale model in 3D of the theatre space with all entrances and exits built into it. A set designer will then build scale models of the set, maybe out of balsa wood or cardboard. The scale used by professional designers is 1:25 – 1cm = 25cm, therefore 4cm = 1metre

Mood board. A mood board is a collage of images, photographs, drawings and words that are your visual response to the key themes and ideas in a play. They are collected on an A3 piece of paper or card as a collage. You might also focus on textures and different types of material and stick these onto your mood board. You might explore the idea of colour on your mood board. These boards are visual responses to key ideas.

Naturalism. This is a meticulous copy of real life or art that tries to reproduce real life. Naturalism attempts to show life as it really is. Soap operas such as *EastEnders* work within the naturalistic genre. It is the dominant form on television today.

Outside eye. Someone who is watching the practical work that you produce and making notes about the characters you begin to create, the narratives you begin to explore and the dialogue that you use. The feedback from the outside eye will be useful as you come to work on your performance.

Practitioner. A practitioner is someone who is working practically in a particular field. A medical practitioner is someone who works practically in the field of medicine; a theatre practitioner is someone who works practically in the field of theatre.

Role on the wall. The most efficient way of creating a character profile is by using a role on the wall. You teacher may ask you to draw the outline of a human figure on a large piece of paper like a gingerbread man in shape. Details about your character are placed within the outline. You can then choose what you record on the outside. In this case, you could identify all the particular pressures that are on that character or the influences that make that character what they are. Your teacher may ask you to record other 'outers'.

Signifier and signified. A signifier is the object itself, for example a clenched fist, and the signified is the meaning the audience read, in this case it may be read as a sign of aggression.

Still image. Sometimes known as a tableau or a more advanced way of referencing this strategy is as a 'depiction'. The action is frozen like a photograph. A still image can allow us to stop the action and to reflect on a specific moment that is frozen. A still image may also be used as a starting point for the drama. Your teacher may ask you to bring the still image to life, or they may ask you to speak the thoughts of the characters in the still image. Think about titling your still image suggesting the political or cultural message that it might contain.

Subtext. Subtext refers to the idea that there is meaning underneath the surface of what is being said or done. The use of subtext creates tension, which in turn creates drama.

Synoptic. Synoptic means having a comprehensive overview of the whole. It may mean having an understanding of the whole play text. It could also mean having an overview of all the explorative strategies and mediums and elements of drama and bringing them all together for this task.

Thought-tracking. You will always thought track in role, as a character. When the role-play is frozen or a still image is created you speak the thought in the character's head. You could thought track yourself or an outside eye could step in and thought track a character.

Total theatre. Total theatre is a style of modern theatre that has been developed from Artaud's ideas. Total theatre combines every theatrical element in an assault on the audience's senses. The term Theatre of Cruelty is another term associated with Artaud, and it is a term that implies theatre should go to the very extremes and become a totally sensory experience for the audience.

Tragedy. Tragedy is a theatrical genre. It is a serious drama in which the action of the play results in suffering or the death of the main characters. A tragedian is an actor who plays tragic roles.

INDEX